Y0-CKL-847

Are You Tired of LIVING?
Biblical Answers for the Hopeless and Despairing

Dr. Lee Roberson

"Dedicated to the memory of
Dr. Herbert Lockyer."

University Publishers
P.O. Box 3571
Chattanooga, Tennessee 37404

Are You Tired of LIVING?
Dr. Lee Roberson

University Publishers

First printing 1945; Copyright renewed 1986 by Dr. Lee Roberson.
ISBN 0-931117-06-2

INTRODUCTION

A few months ago, I had an engagement to speak at the Trinity Baptist Church of Jacksonville, Florida. This great church is pastored by Dr. Bob Gray. On that Sunday evening, it was packed with excited believers. As I came in the door a man stopped me and said, "There is a distinguished gentleman waiting to see you, back of the speaker's platform."

I stepped at once to the rear of the building. There sat Dr. Herbert Lockyer, the noted British Bible teacher and preacher. He was well past 90 years of age but still vigorous and still speaking with a deep, resounding voice. As I saw him that night, my memory went back more than forty years to the time when I brought him to the Highland Park Baptist Church of Chattanooga, Tennessee, for a Bible Conference.

I had never heard anyone just like Dr. Lockyer. Neither had the people of our church. He thrilled us with his messages on prophecy, prayer, the second coming of Christ, and the fullness of the Spirit.

He came to us again in 1946. It was at this time that I felt impressed by the Lord to begin Tennessee Temple Schools. A unanimous vote of the people on July 3, 1946, got the work underway.

Dr. Lockyer gave me much encouragement in the starting of this training institution. I asked him if he would accept the position of vice-president of Tennessee Temple. He agreed to do so, but begged me to remember that he would not be able to be much help locally, but would tell people about the school in various parts of the nation. He did this very faithfully for a limited time.

Back in 1946, Dr. Lockyer insisted that some of my sermons should be put in print. I placed some typed copies of brief messages in his hands. He arranged with his publisher in Philadelphia to finalize the book, with the title, <u>Are You Tired of Living?</u>

This is a re-print of that book. I want to dedicate this volume to the memory of Dr. Herbert Lockyer. The title which he chose was appropriate in that day, but it is more than appropriate in this troubled, confusing, and wicked day.

I trust that this volume will help you.

L.R.

TABLE OF CONTENTS

	PAGE
Are You Tired of Living?	11
The World's Greatest Battle	22
The Vision, the Touch, the Message	31
They Believed	42
The Revival We Need	49
The Rocket Gun of Love	57
Get Wise to Yourself	64
Is Your Life a Hell on Earth?	71
One Way Home	81
The Church Roll and the Lamb's Book of Life	90
Our God—a Consuming Fire	98
The University of Hard Knocks	106
Some Things True of All Men	115
Face to Face	124
The Purple Heart	134
By the Rivers of Babylon	142
Rescued by Angels	154
Your Fortune Told—Free	164
Danger—Deadly Poison	176
The Bible, the Compass of Life	183
700 B. C.	192
"Christians Are Sissies"	200

Dr. Lockyer at age 96
Born Sept. 11, 1886
Died Nov. 30, 1984

FOREWORD

Among the dynamic preachers of the Southern Baptists, Dr. Lee Roberson, of Chattanooga, holds a prominent place. It is seldom that one meets a man who has accomplished so much in so little time. During a visit to his great church in Tennessee, I was greatly impressed with the strong, forceful preaching of Dr. Roberson and had the pleasure of reading many of his messages in his weekly paper. Strongly urged to give them a wider audience, Dr. Roberson consented. Hence this volume.

Here are sermons unique in suggestiveness, direct in their appeal and vibrant with the passion of the Master Dr. Roberson dearly loves.

We predict for this volume an ever increasing circulation among preachers and Christian workers. May it be the forerunner of many more of its kind from the fertile brain and gifted pen of the Highland Park Baptist Church's popular minister.

HERBERT LOCKYER.

Philadelphia, Pa.

ARE YOU TIRED OF LIVING?

"But he himself went a day's journey into the wilderness, and came and sat down under a juniper tree: and he requested for himself that he might die; and said, It is enough: now, O Lord, take away my life; for I am not better than my fathers" (1 K<small>I</small>. 19:4).

There have come times for most of us when life seemed to lose its attractiveness and joy, and death seemed desirable. Life had come to a dead end. It may be that you feel yourself in a "slough of despond." You have lost all zest for living. Your position in life has become unbearable.

Your condition is serious, but it is not incurable. Many others have come to such a place in life. Scores of thousands have found the secret of happy, successful living in the midst of life's deepest despair.

I wish I could help all of you. I wish I could help the folks who are having family difficulties, there is so much of that today. I wish I could help the men who are fighting hard battles with their businesses. I wish I could help the dear folks who are sick of body and afflicted. I would like to be of some help to the young people who are facing so much uncertainty in this time. I'll doubtless fail to touch many cases, but I can help some of you, if you will heed this message.

Let me ask three questions. First, what makes people sometimes long for death? Second, is it right to pray for death? It is not! We are to be ready for death, but we are not to long for it. Life is God-given. We should handle it as a divine gift. We should use it as a trust. It is to be developed. Third, do men pray for death? I give you two from the Bible. Elijah is the first. After an enormous victory on Mt. Carmel, when God sent down fire from Heaven; after a victory over the priests and prophets of Baal; after God had sent down an abundance of rain after three and a half years of drought, we find Elijah praying to die. What a picture he makes! He is sitting under a tree and saying, "O Lord, take away my life; for I am not better than my fathers" (1 Ki. 19:4). He requested for himself that he might die.

What was wrong? He was afraid for his life and disgusted with his cowardice. When Elijah killed the prophets of Baal, who belonged to Jezebel, she sent a messenger to Elijah saying that by the next day he would be as dead as her prophets. When Elijah heard that, he started running and didn't stop until he got to Beersheba, a hundred miles away. You say that surely was some running. Yes it was, but many men have run farther than that when some woman got after them. He left his servant there and went a day's journey into the wilderness. There we see him praying for death. He is blowing like a horse with the heaves. The perspiration is running off his body. He is scared, tired and disgusted; so he says, "Lord, let me die."

That is getting down pretty low, but here is where the story turns. Elijah was God's man, God's child, and now in the midst of gloom and despondency, God comes and touches him and gives to him renewal of strength and sends him back to fight the battle. God will do the same for you if you will let Him. He may not speak in the strong wind, the earthquake, or the fire; but after all that will come the still small voice. Listen for it and heed it.

There is another character in the Bible who prayed to die. Life became unbearable to him for quite a different reason than Elijah's. His name was Jonah. His life was a series of "ups and downs" until he obediently went to Nineveh and preached. A whole city of 600,000 turned to God under his preaching and God showed mercy and spared them all. This so peeved Jonah that he prayed, "Therefore now, O Lord, take, I beseech Thee, my life from me; for it is better for me to die than to live" (Jon. 4:3).

What was wrong with him? He did not understand God's ways. He did not understand God's will and purpose. Many folks are going to be in that predicament before this war is over. They are going to be mad at God, mad and peeved because they do not understand His plan. The big Christian, the happy Christian in this day, is the one who says, "Not mine to reason why." Keep on trusting, keep on believing, and life's mysteries will one day be explained.

So much for the two great men of old who prayed to die.

Now, what is it that makes life worth living? What makes for successful, happy living? What must we have to get the most out of life?

I

THERE MUST BE VISION

The writer of Proverbs says, "Where there is no vision, the people perish; but he that keepeth the law, happy is he" (Prov. 29:18). Right there is the reason why many people find life unhappy and unbearable.

They have no goal in life. Life is an aimless ramble, made up of the same humdrum experiences day after day. There is no joy of achievement. They are not heading for a definite destination in life.

Many have no vision of good to be done. Life is a constant selfish procedure; receiving everything but giving nothing. Life loses its thrill and its joy when you are living for self! There is the sin of our Christian forces. Men are saved by the glorious grace of God and then live on in utter selfishness. Men and women rob God and expect to have joy in their hearts.

Get a vision of what you ought to be doing. Say good-bye to selfishness. The Lord will help you to conquer that sin; you can't do it by yourself. Your worst enemy is yourself. When Abraham Lincoln was candidate for the presidency, someone asked him what he thought of the prospect. With characteristic humor, he answered, "I do not fear Breckenridge, for he is of the South, and the North will not support him; I do not fear Douglas for the South is against him. But there is a man named Lincoln I see in the papers of whom I am very much afraid. If I am defeated, it will be by that man."

Get a vision of the dying multitudes of this earth, dying without Christ. W. W. Martin tells of putting these words over the clock in a certain mission church: "83 a minute." At last a group came to him and said, "Will you kindly take that down? It haunts us." They knew that it meant that 83 souls a minute were passing into eternity, into the dark. Most of them had never heard about Jesus Christ.

Get a vision of unselfish service to others. A number of outstanding people of this city were asked to answer the question, Give three rules for successful, happy living. Almost every reply said in substance, "Live for others." Hear them: "Witness for the Lord. Winning others to Christ brings the greatest joy in life." That came from a prominent school man. "Unselfish living brings great joy." That came from a business man. "Engage in some labor most beneficial to your fellowman."

You know why you are so tired of living? You are in a rut and "a rut is a grave with both ends knocked out."

II
THERE MUST BE VIGOR FOR LIFE

There must be enthusiasm for life. Paul says, "Not slothful in business; fervent in spirit; serving the Lord" (Rom. 12:11). The apostle believed in putting his best into every task. Too many folks are licked before they begin. They go at their jobs in a half-hearted fashion.

I can usually tell when a man is going to make a success in doing a certain task. If his body is alert, and his eye has a sparkle and if he is sort of leaning forward, anxious, ready, and enthusiastic, he is going to do something. He may make a lot of mistakes, but he is going to win out. But if a man slumps around, if his eye is dull, and he holds back and delays starting at the job, he's licked before he starts. Too many folks break the backing straps anyway.

In the last few years I have read many books of biography. I like to read about folks and how they win in life's battles. I found three things to be true of all who triumph.

1. The world's great achieve in spite of handicaps; you might even say because of handicaps. The world's great have been men and women who started out with tremendous

handicaps. You might not know it when you see them at the top of the ladder, but it is so.

Homer endured blindness and experienced poverty of the direst sort, but he went on to lead the company of the world's great poets. Shakespeare was unfortunate enough to be born in the home of a bankrupt butcher and a mother who could not write her own name, yet his hard life became a high school for him. Beethoven was born in poverty. His father was a drunkard and his mother sick, but he rose to the heights of harmony and his music charms the world.

Faraday, one of the great scientists of the world, was born in a stable; his father was a blacksmith in poverty-stricken circumstances. Helen Keller had to win out over blindness, deafness, and dumbness. She kept on tenaciously. The world bows at her feet. Demosthenes had to overcome an awful impediment in his speech, but he practiced on the seashore with pebbles in his mouth until he became the world's greatest orator.

The world's great achieve in spite of handicaps.

2. The world's great refuse to let despondency disturb progress. Even in the midst

of discouragement and darkness they keep on going. Men are going to oppose you at times. Your heart will be broken a thousand times because of the unfaithfulness and fickleness of men. But we must not allow despondency and disappointment to slow down our progress and our growth.

3. The world's great have erased the words "I quit" from their vocabularies. They kept on plugging away. I heard Dr. Lee preach one time on the "Glory of Keeping At It," and it is without doubt those who have achieved in life who have vigorously and enthusiastically kept at the job. If life is going to have meaning, if it is going to be worth while, put your best into it.

III

There Must Be Victory Over Sin if You Are to Live Happily and Successfully

You may have vision and yet fail if you don't have the victory over sin. You may have vigor and enthusiasm, but if sin comes in, you are ruined. You may have splendid training and education for life and still fail miserably if sin comes into your heart to reign.

Child of God, if you want victory over sin,

keep your eyes on Jesus. This world will tempt, trouble and trip you, but Jesus can give you the victory.

Some unknown author has told the story of a king, one of whose subjects asked him the question: "How may I escape yielding to temptation?"

The king answered, "Take this vessel brimful of oil and carry it to the outskirts of the city and back without spilling one drop, and you will learn the lesson; but remember if one drop is spilled, your head comes off." He sent two executioners to follow him every step of the way with drawn swords to carry out his order should there be occasion.

Now, it happened that there was a Fair going on in the town, and the streets were crowded, making the experiment far more difficult and dangerous, but by extreme pains the man returned, the executioners following him to report, "He spilled not a drop."

"Whom did you see while you went through the streets?" the king asked the man.

"No one," answered the man. "I was so intent upon not spilling a drop of oil that I noticed nothing else."

"Then," said the king, "you know now how

to avoid temptation. Keep your mind as firmly on God, and the sights of sin and their alluring calls will not even be noticed by you."

Lost friend, look to Christ for victory. You cannot save yourself. Reformation is futile without Christ. Christ is the only way of salvation. "There is none other name under Heaven given among men, whereby we must be saved" (Acts 4:12). For six thousand years men have sought to help themselves but have failed. Christ alone has the words of eternal life.

Friend in sin, if you want happiness and victory, settle that sin account now.

When Henry Blunt was dying, the doctor said to him, "Sir, you are drawing near the grave, and I think if you have any accounts to settle, you had better settle them now." Mr. Blunt replied, "I have no accounts to settle; I owe nothing to man, and my Saviour has paid all my debts to God!" Can you say the same? If not, turn to Jesus now, and to the joy of the knowledge of sins forgiven will be added a new joy in living and a new zest for life.

THE WORLD'S GREATEST BATTLE

No one, except the most bloodthirsty, enjoys talking about war and big battles. And yet, this is the subject most frequently upon the lips of men and women today. It is the subject of thousands of books. It is the theme of all news broadcasts and many radio programs. The war of today touches the person living in the most remote section of America. In days gone by many people could live and be scarcely aware that a war was in progress, but not so today.

The year 1944 will be long remembered. In it, great and decisive battles were fought. The history books will record the momentous events of this year for the children of the future to read. The story will be thrilling, for the study of great battles is an interesting one.

It was a great and unusual battle when Joshua defeated Amalek as Aaron and Hur held up the arms of Moses. The story is recorded in Exodus 17.

It was a great battle when Joshua and his army of five thousand defeated and slew the inhabitants of Ai, even 12,000 people. This battle is described in Joshua 8.

It was a great battle when Gideon and his

little band of 300 men under the guidance of God defeated the Midianites, as we are told in Judges 6.

It was a great and bloody battle when the Philistines slew some 34,000 of the Jews at almost one time. This is recorded in 1 Samuel 4.

It was a short and decisive battle when David, with his sling and some round rocks killed Goliath, the Philistine, and removed the yoke of bondage from his people.

It was a great battle when the Israelites fought the Syrians and killed 100,000 footmen in one day (1 Ki. 20:29). And then a wall fell on 27,000 more of the Syrians and killed them.

The world has known many great and bloody battles.

In the battle of Eylau, February 7, 1807, Napoleon lost 23,150 men, the Russians lost 26,000 men; 49,150 losses in one day.

At Waterloo, the French lost 14,000 men killed; and six thousand wounded, who were captured by the British.

In single battles of World War 1, scores of thousands were killed. In the defense of Verdun, the French alone had 410,000 casualties.

But remarkable as are these records and

stupendous as is the scale upon which modern war is waged, the world's greatest and most decisive battle has not yet been fought and it will not be fought this year. When will it be fought? It will be fought after the world's greatest depression. That depression is called in the Word "the great tribulation." The battle is called "the battle of Armageddon." The tribulation will last for seven years, and the world's greatest battle will come at the close.

I want to give you three reasons for saying that this is the world's greatest battle in numbers and decisiveness.

I

It Is the World's Greatest Battle Because of the Participants

Who will engage in this battle? The answer can quickly be given: The whole world.

On one side will be the armies of this earth under the leadership of the world dictator and the false prophet. They are energized by the devil himself. The beast of Revelation is the world dictator. The false prophet is his miracle working partner.

In the battle of Armageddon, the forces which come against Jerusalem come forth from the whole earth. "I will gather all nations and will bring them down into the valley Jehoshaphat: and I will execute judgment upon them there" (Joel 3:2).

"I will gather all nations against Jerusalem to battle . . . Then shall Jehovah go forth, and fight against those nations. And His feet shall stand in that day upon the mount of Olives, which is before Jerusalem on the east" (Zech. 14:2-4).

In this battle there will be the most magnificent array of military power the world has ever seen. "For they are the spirits of devils, working miracles, which go forth unto the kings of the earth and of the whole world, to gather them to the battle of that great day of God Almighty . . . And He gathered them together into a place called in the Hebrew tongue Armageddon" (Rev. 16:14-16)

Now see the picture: On one side, the kings of the earth with the beast of Revelation as commander-in-chief. On the other side the picture is simple but glorious. It is found in Revelation 19:11-21. Christ and His saints come to make war against the beast and his armies. See Christ as He comes clothed in a vesture dipped in blood. He comes as the King of kings and the Lord of lords.

II
It Is the World's Greatest Battle Because Its Awfulness Exceeds All Others

In loss of life and bloody conflict, Armageddon is the world's greatest. When I say that, I am taking into account the terrible wars and battles which the world has seen.

All the inventive genius and war strategy of man will come to a head and climax in the battle of Armageddon. In this connection, it is interesting to notice the tragic increase in man's ability to deal out death.

In the Seven Years War of 1756 to 1763, a war with Prussia and Great Britain against Austria, France, Russia and others, Austria lost 303,000; Prussia lost 180,000; Russia about 50,000.

In the wars of Napoleon, between 1805–15, 370,750 were killed, 964,000 were wounded: a total of 1,334,750.

In the Franco-Prussian War of 1870–71, France lost 280,000 men.

In the Civil War of 1861–65, the North lost about 275,000 men, the South about the same number. Something over one half million were killed or died from wounds.

In World War 1 between ten and eleven millions of military personnel were killed or died.

The complete total of this present conflict will not be known, perhaps for years. But the present war and the wars of the past will seem as children's picnics compared to the tribulation and the battle of Armageddon at its close.

In World War 1, about ten million men lost their lives.

Revelation 9:18 tells us that one third of all mankind will die in the time of the end; seventy times the number of World War 1, roughly around 600,000,000.

In the battle of Armageddon 200 million soldiers will take part (Rev. 9:16), and the battle's awfulness is described in Revelation 9:16-19.

This will be the bloodiest time of all history. Blood two feet deep flowed in the streets of Jerusalem in A. D. 70 when Titus the Roman conqueror wrecked the city of Jerusalem. But in the battle of Armageddon, the Word says, "And the winepress was trodden without the city, and blood came out of the winepress, even unto the horse bridles, by the space of a thousand and six hundred furlongs" (Rev. 14: 20). A furlong is 582 feet.

III

IT IS THE WORLD'S GREATEST BATTLE BECAUSE OF ITS OUTCOME

The beast (the dictator) and the false prophet are cast alive into Hell. They have had their little day. And now they enter the abode of all Christ-rejectors.

Satan comes to his Waterloo. Throughout the ages Satan has been victorious. Sin and the devil's agents have had their way. But after the battle of Armageddon, Satan is chained in the abyss. His power is taken from the earth. If there is any passage hated by Satan, it is Revelation 20:1-3.

This battle will bring to an end world conflicts. Men have often asked, "Why doesn't God stop this war?" One of these days He is going to stop war. Armageddon will bring to an end the bloody reign of sinful man; it will bring in the peaceful reign of the sinless Christ.

This battle brings victory to Christ. Nineteen hundred years ago they slapped the Son of God in the face, scourged Him, and crowned

Him with a crown of thorns. Nineteen hundred years ago they spit in His face and nailed Him to a cross. But when He returns to earth again, there will be a different story.

When "the great tribulation" is at its worst; when the antichrist, the false prophet and all the forces of evil are arrayed together in one great army under the personal leadership of Satan, Christ Himself will return to earth accompanied by God's army.

God's army is mightier than all the combined armies of all the nations of the world. Christ and His army are pictured in Revelation 19. When the smoke of the battle rolls away, Jesus the Christ, Son of David, Lion of the Tribe of Judah, will stand alone in power and glory. He will speak peace to the nations that are left, and sorrow and sighing will flee away.

And then Christ will be King, and we shall reign with Him, forever. Are you going to be there?

> When the saints go marching in
> When the saints go marching in,
> Lord, I want to be in that number
> When the saints go marching in.

It depends on what you do with Christ.

Accept His death on the cross. He died to take away your sin. He died in your place.

An African chief, listening to a missionary's recital of the gospel story, in sudden comprehension, leaped to his feet and shouted, "Come down! Come down from that cross! I tell You, You have no business there! That's my place!"

"Who His own self bare our sins in His own body on the tree, that we, being dead to sins, should live unto righteousness: by whose stripes ye were healed" (1 Pet. 2:24). Accept Him today! Let Him, by His power, fight life's greatest battle, the battle of sin, for you, so that you may be on His side, the victory side, when the world's greatest battle is finished.

THE VISION—THE TOUCH—THE MESSAGE

"And when I saw Him, I fell at His feet as dead. And He laid His right hand upon me, saying unto me, Fear not; I am the first and the last; I am He that liveth, and was dead; and behold I am alive forevermore, Amen; and have the keys of hell and of death" (REV. 1:17-18).

There are some things which happen to us within the span of twenty four hours which completely change our lives. Some lives are blasted by sudden and unexpected happenings, the happenings of a single day. Some lives are deepened spiritually by the unexpected occurrences of life.

In a certain city, there is a very fine pastor whose life is a blessing and inspiration to thousands. Twenty five years ago his beautiful young wife was taken from him by death. At her death he made a complete and unreserved consecration of himself to God. He has never forgotten his wife, and he has never forgotten his pledge to God. Each Sunday her envelope, along with his, is placed in the offering plate. A friend of mine saw the envelopes one Sunday;

each of them contained twenty five dollars. He gives away all his money. He has given his life to God.

Yes, there are things which can happen in the span of a single day which can never be forgotten in eternity. The day I accepted Christ an eternal transaction was made. All of my life here, and all my life to come will be touched by the act of that day when I was an Intermediate boy.

Again, there are decisions made in a single day which will blight and damn for eternity. Aaron Burr took a certain time to decide whether he would be a Christian or not. The day he decided against Christ blighted all hope for eternity and procured his eternal damnation in the pit of hell.

John, the disciple whom Jesus loved, had an experience on a certain day, the like of which no one else has ever had. He said, "I was in the Spirit on the Lord's day . . ." And then to John was given a vision, a divine touch, and a message.

I
The Vision
"And when I saw Him, I fell at His feet as

The Vision, the Touch, the Message 33

dead." For this vision we must read the verses just before (Rev. 1:13-16). He saw the Christ, the Son of God. He saw Jesus in priestly robes and kingly glory walking among the churches, and when he did, he fell at His feet as dead.

He saw the Lord:

"Clothed with a garment down to the foot," the spotless righteousness of Christ, covering from head to foot.

"His head and His hairs were white like wool, as white as snow . . ." This showed the Christ as the Ancient of Days.

"His eyes were as a flame of fire." His eyes were piercing and penetrating, seeing all and knowing all. When He was here in the flesh His eyes were tender, but here they are penetrating.

"His feet like unto fine brass, as if they burned in a furnace." This represents the Master's suffering. He was made perfect through suffering.

"His voice as the sound of many waters," comforting to the believer, thunders of judgment to the unbeliever.

"And He had in His right hand seven stars; and out of His mouth went a sharp twoedged sword; and His countenance was as the sun shining in His strength," a glorious vision of the

Christ even exceeding that of the mount of transfiguration. And you remember John was present on that day.

What happened when John saw the vision? "I fell at His feet as dead."

When we see Jesus, we do no boasting of our goodness. In the light of His presence our imperfections stand out in bold relief.

One should be wary of that fellow who goes around talking about how good he is, and what he does and what he doesn't do. No Christian is going to brag and boast when standing in the presence of Jesus and seeing His holiness.

The Christian needs to be humble. A clear vision of Christ will keep him humble. I heard an outstanding evangelist of world renown begin boasting about how good he was and his revival froze up and never broke. The people knew something was wrong. There is something wrong when we boast of our goodness. Our story is

> Amazing grace, how sweet the sound,
>   That saved a wretch like me;
> I once was lost, but now am found,
>   Was blind, but now I see.

When the lost man sees Christ, he sees his own need. It is easy to see how the lost world can sit back and boast about morality and good works and at the same time reject Christ. They have never seen Him! Stand up beside the sinless, stainless, holy Christ, and you will drop to your knees and cry for forgiveness. Then you will say, "O, Lord, be merciful to me a sinner, and save my soul for Jesus' sake."

You may say that you are not such a bad sinner. That does not matter; it takes just as much grace to save the vilest. If you have broken one law, you have broken them all. If one wheel is broken in a watch, it won't go. If you were hanging over a precipice by a chain of one hundred links and someone smashed all the links, where would you go? To the bottom, of course! But suppose just one link were broken, where would you go? To the bottom!

Seeing Jesus, you see yourself as a sinner, and when you do, something is going to happen.

II
The Touch

"And He laid His right hand upon me." Not His left hand, but the right hand of authority; Jesus placed His right hand, nail-scarred, upon John.

There are times when we need the touch of a

friendly hand, a hand of encouragement, a hand of power.

There are days so dark that I seek in vain
   For the face of my Friend Divine;
But though darkness hide, He is there to guide,
   By the touch of His hand on mine.

When the way is dim, and I cannot see
   Through the mist of His wise design,
How my glad heart yearns and my faith returns,
   By the touch of His hand on mine.

Oh, the touch of His hand on mine,
   Oh, the touch of His hand on mine,
There is grace and power, in the trying hour,
   In the touch of His hand on mine.

Do you remember the children's song—

I think when I read that sweet story of old,
   When Jesus was here among men,
How He called little children as lambs to His fold,
   I should like to have been with them then.

I wish that His hands had been placed on my head

That His arms had been thrown around me,
And that I might have seen His kind look when
  He said,
"Let the little ones come unto Me."

When John could not stand the brightness of the vision, the Lord in kindness placed His right hand upon Him. In the touch of Jesus there is love. In the touch of Christ there is power. When we are separated from Him we are powerless, we are overpowered; but when He touches, we are empowered.

III
The Message

"Fear not; I am the first and the last; I am He that liveth, and was dead; and behold I am alive forevermore, Amen; and have the keys of Hades and of death."

Listen, troubled Christian, to this message from the Christ.

Listen, uncertain Christian, fearful of your security, Christ has something to say to you.

Listen, lost friend, to the Christ. Disregard the words of the world and listen to God. What a message for dying men!

"Fear not!" The world is a cesspool of fear. Men's hearts are failing them because of fear;

fear of man, fear of death, fear of the future.

"I am the first and the last." Before the sun or stars were made Christ was. When the sun and stars will shine no more, Christ will be.

Before dictators and kings, Christ was. When dictators and kings shall be no more, Christ remains.

Again, He says, "I am alive forevermore." They nailed Him to a cross, they put Him to a cruel death, but He lives! Forevermore!

There is no power in earth or hell which can take Jesus from the right hand of God, and bring Him back, disrobe Him, spit on Him, put a crown of thorns upon Him, nail Him to a cross, and have Him bleed to death and then bury Him. All of that is over. Christ is alive forevermore, and because He lives, I shall live also. We can know that we have eternal life because of Him.

Christ says, "I have the keys of Hades and of death." He controls all. No pope or priest has the keys; Jesus has them. I once passed by the Shrine of the Little Flower of Father Coughlin, just outside Detroit. The building cost more than two million dollars. He represents a church which teaches that it has the keys of hell and death. The keys are not there,

Jesus has them. All things are in the hands of the Son. All power is His. All love and mercy belong to Him.

That is my message, *a living Christ;* not a dead Christ, not a Christ of the tomb, but a Saviour alive forevermore. Therefore, fear not; neither fear this life nor the life to come. He is all in all, He is the first and the last, and He holds the keys.

He is coming one of these days, for He said, "I will come again, and receive you unto Myself, that where I am there ye may be also." Lift up your eyes, look for Him, and look to the home beyond.

Someone tells the story of a little boy playing in the sands along the seashore. He was building a city in the sand. He laid out the streets, built the houses, stores, banks, churches, and homes. And with childish fancy he placed around his modern community an ancient city wall. Outside the city he laid out highways, farms and farmhouses. All afternoon he worked, building his city. He did not notice that the sun was setting, that the clouds were gathering, that the wind was growing chill. He was too busy with his city. He did not notice that the tide was coming in, the waves mounting higher and higher, until one wave, mightier than the rest, came sweeping in about him, washing away his houses and his lands, his city and his farms. In fright, the little child ran back against the cliff, alone and afraid.

But above him on the cliff sat his older brother. He had seen it all. He had watched his younger brother play in the sand, had seen the larger wave wash away his houses and lands; he had noticed his brother's fright and distress. He reached down the cliff and caught hold of the hand of his younger brother, and pulled him up to safety. Then with his arm about him, they faced away from the tide and the sea, and walked together toward the open door of the brightly lighted home of their father.

And so we play upon the sands of time, building our cities, our houses and lands. So intent do we become that we do not notice that the evening draws near, that the clouds are filling the sky, that the tide is coming in, and that soon all our little efforts to build earthly things will be washed away. And when the tides of misfortune, of sadness, or of death do strike, like the small boy, we are terrified.

But above is our Elder Brother. He has seen it all, as once He experienced it. He reaches down His hand, catches hold of our hand, and lifts us up. Putting His arm about us, we turn from this bourne of time and place toward the open door of that heavenly home.

My friend, may you at this moment see Jesus, feel the touch of His hand, and receive His glorious message.

THEY BELIEVED

"And ye shall receive power, after that the Holy Ghost is come upon you: and ye shall be witnesses unto Me both in Jerusalem, and in all Judea, and in Samaria, and unto the uttermost part of the earth" (ACTS 1:8).

The world has never ceased to marvel at the wonderful story of Christian progress in the first century. Today there is a crying need for all our churches and denominations to go back and study the methods, the messages, and the men of the first century. The history of the Prodigal Son is pretty much the history of the church. Now that she "begins to be in want," she must needs "arise and go back" to her original sphere of power and prestige. What did the early saints believe? How did they live? How did they work? How did they preach and testify? How did they die?

In the midst of our present day failures, we need to look back. We cannot depend upon what the seminaries teach, nor on what modernists believe. Many of our modern leaders and teachers have gone a long way from the New Testament way of doing things. For example, a seminary recently brought a northern modernist to that seminary for a series of lectures. One of the asinine things he said to the almost five hundred preachers was: "You should not preach more than once per Sunday if you can help. No man can preach more than one great sermon per Sunday." Some of the preachers thought it was great stuff. Who cares about the greatness of the sermon? We are trying to win souls. I am sure that one of the curses of our modern pulpit is the attempt of too many preachers to preach *great* sermons.

Now, let us look back to the first century and the story of the early saints.

I
THEY BELIEVED

After the resurrection and Pentecost their beliefs turned as hard as concrete.

They believed in the divinity of Christ. "But ye denied the Holy One and the Just and desired a murderer to be granted unto you; and killed the Prince of Life, whom God hath raised from the dead; whereof we are witnesses" (Acts 3:14, 15).

Let the skeptics and infidels believe what they will, let nothing shake you from the fact that

Christ by many infallible proofs showed Himself to be the divine Son of God.

They believed in the atoning work of Christ. "Take heed therefore unto yourselves, and to all the flock, over the which the Holy Ghost hath made you overseers, to feed the church of God, which He hath purchased with His own blood" (Acts 20:28).

They believed that Christ died for our sins according to the Scriptures. They believed that only through the shed blood of Christ could man be made at one with God.

They believed in the presence of Christ. "Then spake the Lord to Paul in the night by a vision, Be not afraid, but speak, and hold not thy peace; for I am with thee, and no man shall set on thee to hurt thee . . ." (Acts 18:9, 10).

Later we see Paul writing to the Galatians, "I am crucified with Christ; nevertheless, I live, yet not I but Christ liveth in me." Christ was with them in all they did for Him.

II

They Testified of Christ and His Salvation

Three things characterized the testimonies of the early saints.

The first thing is courage. They had courage to preach and teach doctrines which were despised.

They had courage to rebuke sin in high places. In Acts 4 and 5 you find the apostle Peter bravely speaking before the priests, the Roman military officials, and the Pharisees and the Sadducees. They had courage to declare the whole counsel of God: "for we cannot but speak the things which we have seen and heard" (Acts 4:20).

Their testimony was positive.

There was no uncertain sound about it. They testified in plain and unmistakable words to the life, death and resurrection of Christ. They said that He was the only way of salvation. "Neither is there salvation in any other; for there is none other name under heaven given among men, whereby we must be saved" (Acts 4:12).

May God give us positive testimonies.

They testified with power.

It was not the power of society. It was not the power of money. "Silver and gold have I none, but such as I have give I thee." It was not the power of intellect. "Now when they saw the boldness of Peter and John, and perceived that they were unlearned and ignorant men, they marvelled; and they took knowledge of them, that they had been with Jesus" (Acts 4:13).

It was the power of the Holy Spirit. Their testimonies empowered by the Spirit brought men to conviction and salvation. We need Christians whose testimony is courageous, positive, and powerful.

III

They Suffered and Died for Christ

Here is a part of the story we like to skip over. But you cannot avoid it when you study the lives of the early saints.

They suffered for Christ. They suffered ridicule, criticism. They suffered the loss of their homes and loved ones. They suffered the shame of imprisonment. They suffered untold hardships to tell the story of Christ. Everywhere there were such experiences as those of Paul given in 2 Corinthians 11:23–27.

Today we suffer so little for Christ. If we are criticized, we want to quit. If the work of Christ is in need, we sacrifice little or none. Few of us have ever missed a meal for the sake of Christ. Few of us have ever given up the purchase of new clothing for the sake of Christ. They died for Christ.

I give you one glorious account. A deacon in the first church in Jerusalem stood up and preached a sermon. He was stoned to death by the enemies of the Christ. But he died victoriously; and like Elijah of old, his mantle of power fell upon the shoulders of Saul, who became Paul, the mighty preacher.

Think of the dying of the apostles:

"Matthew perished at the edge of the sword. Mark died as a result of being dragged through the streets of Alexandria. Luke was hanged upon an olive tree in the classic land of Greece. St. John was flung first into a boiling pot, and though saved in a miraculous manner, was afterward banished to the Isle of Patmos. Peter was crucified at Rome with his head down. James was beheaded at Jerusalem. Philip Bartholomew was flayed alive. Andrew perished on a cross. St. Thomas was pierced by a lance. Matthias was stoned and beheaded. Paul perished by beheading in Rome, and Jude was shot to death with arrows. These were the men who loved not their lives to the death."

Are we better than the men who suffered and died for Jesus? May God help us to be true to Christ, even though it means suffering, ridicule, scoffing, and even death.

The early church made more progress than we, because it was more prodigal of the lives of men. Suffering, persecution, and death scattered the blaze of gospel fire. Whether in life or death we shall not be separated from the love of God which is in Christ Jesus our Lord.

When Roland Hill, the great English preacher, was 84, and just before his death, one Sunday night after the lights had been put out in the church, he was heard walking up and down the aisles of the dark church singing:

When I am to die, receive me I'll cry,
For Jesus has loved me, I cannot tell why;
But this I do find, we two are so joined,
He'll not be in heaven and leave me behind.

Every soul can sing that who has believed, who has testified to Christ and His salvation, and if need be, has suffered and died for Him.

THE REVIVAL WE NEED

"Wilt thou not revive us again; that Thy people may rejoice in Thee?" (Psa. 85:6).

Any person coming into our city would doubtless be moved to say, "I perceive that in all things you are a very religious people."

Ours is surely a town of many churches. Within a very few blocks there are more than a dozen church buildings. Some of the churches are large, some small, some are rich and some are poor, some growing and some at a standstill, but one thing is true of all churches: we need a revival!

May we let this prayer of the Psalmist go up from our hearts today, "Wilt thou not revive us again?"

Allow me to suggest the kind of revival I believe we need.

I

We Need a Revival of Bible Teaching and Preaching

All about us there is great confusion on cardinal fundamental Bible doctrines. The people are uncertain and untaught.

There is, first of all, confusion about the way of salvation. Question a few people on the way of salvation and you will see the need of a revival of Bible teaching and preaching.

You will find many who will say, "I used to be a Christian, but I'm not now." Such a person needs to be taught the Word. Another will say in answer to the question, Are you a Christian?, "I am trying to be" or "I'm doing the best I know how." Now, some of these uncertain individuals may be saved but the devil is getting the best of such testimonies.

Take one hundred church members of any of our churches and over one half of them will give indefinite, uncertain answers. Many such people need to know Christ and all of them need to know the Word of God.

Inside of our church rolls there is a great evangelistic field. Our church rolls and the Lamb's Book of Life are not the same.

Many names have been added to our church rolls which have never been added to the Lamb's Book of Life. Plain Bible teaching and preaching will help us to win many who have never been regenerated. Many preachers are so afraid to repeat themselves that in many services the way of salvation is not made clear.

I was assisting a pastor in one of our large southern churches a few years ago. I was leading the music. He was a good preacher, but I will never forget what he said on the second night of the meeting. After I had finished the song service, he stood up to bring the message and in a very apologetic tone, he said, "My friends, I'm going to speak tonight on Regeneration. As you know, it is my custom to use this theme about once every year."

If we are going to make sure that folks who come forth to unite with our churches are saved, we better preach, "Ye must be born again" every Sunday. If you feel led to preach on "Debt free in '43" or the Red Cross, or the War Chest, or some other laudable object, then we better hold the audience fifteen minutes longer and present the plain way of salvation.

In addition to confusion about the way of salvation, there is likewise much confusion about obedience to Bible commands after regeneration. We need a revival of Bible teaching and preaching to let people know that if they love the Lord, they will keep His commands. They will confess their faith in Him, follow Him in baptism, and then go out to witness for Him.

Again, there is much confusion about what constitutes a New Testament church. Multitudes of folks will say, and they apparently believe it, "One church is just as good as another." That is not so, but such a conception leads many into churches where Christ is not lifted up and proclaimed as the only way of salvation. And notice, if salvation is by grace and grace alone, we are in the midst of a great untouched evangelistic field. On every side of you there are churches preaching and teaching salvation by good works, baptism, and church membership.

Yes, we need a revival of Bible teaching and preaching. May preachers and people be stirred and sent out proclaiming the Word of God boldly.

II

We Need a Revival Which Will Set Us on Fire for the Souls of Men

This sounds old, time-worn, and trite, but it is what we need. Our interest in soul winning has been as spasmodic as it has been indifferent. Our churches need to be filled with a Christlike compassion for the lost. "Not just a fever for numbers, but a real passion for souls."

Our people must separate themselves from sin that we might have power to witness. Too many of our people are unable to be soul winners because of worldly alliances. They have no power as Christians.

Indifference must be purged from our lives. We must be in dead earnest about the souls of men. They are lost and condemned *now*. We must tell them *now*.

John Vassar, of days gone by, was walking down the street with a pastor. The pastor pointed to a blacksmith shop and said, "The old blacksmith over there is not a Christian. If it comes handy for you while you are here, I wish you would speak to him about his soul." Vassar said, "I will go and speak to him now." In less than ten minutes, the blacksmith had released the foot of the horse he was shoeing and was down on his knees by the anvil asking God to save him.

We must be daring in our efforts to win to Christ. The apostles spoke with boldness. Paul was daring. Great soul winners have been people courageous and unafraid.

III

WE NEED A REVIVAL OF BELIEVING PRAYER

We proclaim to the world that we believe in prayer, yet we pray but little. We recognize our need of prayer, yet we pray but little. We quote the promises of the Bible on prayer, but we do not claim them for ourselves. If the Lord were to answer some of our prayers, it would scare us to death. We pray so often without any idea of an answer and certainly not a sudden or miraculous answer.

Some of you have been praying a long time for loved ones and friends. Pray more earnestly in these days for their conviction and salvation; the time of victory may be near. I know we get discouraged, but this may be the time of victory.

A wife came forward in one of my meetings. She said, "I heard what you said about prayer, but I'm ready to quit. I have prayed twelve years for my husband. During this time I have tried to serve God faithfully. My husband is an awful sinner—drinks, and everything that goes with it. I have a letter here from my mother and father asking me to come home to them. I have tried long enough."

"Let's pray on for a few days longer," I said. "Don't give up just yet."

In that very meeting that husband came forward and accepted Christ. I have been in the home; it is one of the happiest Christian homes in that city. May we pray as we have not prayed before. May we keep on asking, seeking, and knocking.

George Muller, that prince of intercessors with God, began to pray for a group of five personal friends. After five years, one of them came to Christ. In ten years, two more of them found peace in the Saviour. He prayed on for twenty five years and the fourth man was saved. For the fifth man he prayed until the time of his death, and this friend came to Christ a few months after George Muller died. For this last friend he had prayed almost fifty two years.

But, thank God, ofttimes prayer is answered much quicker than that. A mother deeply burdened in a revival for her son stayed in the church all night and prayed for that son who lived in a city some distance away. All night long she knocked at the door of prayer. Along toward morning she felt that the victory was won. Without breakfast or sleep she came to the 10 o'clock service and a few minutes later her son walked in. That morning he was saved. When asked why he came home, he said that the night before, after twelve, he had a strange dream and the impression that he should go home at once. He came home, found the revival going on, came to the service and was saved. The impression that brought him home came during the time that his mother was on her knees in the old country church praying for him.

A revival of Bible teaching and preaching!
A revival of witnessing!
A revival of believing prayer!
This we need!

THE ROCKET GUN OF LOVE

"If ye love Me, keep My Commandments" (JOHN 14:15).

The dictionary says, "A rocket is a cylindrical tube containing combustibles which on being ignited liberate gases whose action propels the tube through the air."

In this present war the rocket gun is one of the most destructive pieces of firearms used. But a rocket can also be used for life-saving. A rocket can carry a life line out to a drowning man. But it has to be touched off first. There must be a force which drives the rocket out and on.

Now, in the soul winning business, the average Christian is not going out to win others until he is sent out by a driving force. The preacher can hand out cards and beg and plead but that does not last. A revival may stir you for a while and then the effect of that disappears. The death of a loved one may give you a spurt of spiritual energy and then the effect wears off. And so, I want to give you three things, which, if exploded in your brain and heart, will make you a soul winner for all time to come.

I
The First Is Love

Primarily it is our love for Him. "We love Him because He first loved us." "If ye love Me, keep My commandments." Oh, how that digs into our hearts. I would not want a person to walk up to me and say, "You don't love Christ." And yet, Jesus must feel that you do not love Him because you fail to keep His commandments.

Our love should drive us out in service for Him. There is an old proverb which says, "He who has love in his heart has spurs in his side." As we love Christ more we will serve more. I am sure this was the driving force in the ministry of the apostles. They knew the Christ. They loved Him so. "For Jesus' sake" they endured all hardships. Their love for Him was sufficient motive to keep them going for him.

Second, our love for others should drive us out in witnessing. Our love for the souls of men should make us restless to go.

What miracles can be wrought by Christian love! A Christian woman went to a tract house in New York and asked for tracts for distribution. The first day she was out on her

Christian errand she saw a policeman taking an intoxicated woman to the station house. After the woman was discharged from custody, the Christian woman saw her coming away, all unkempt and unlovely. She went up, threw her arms about her neck and kissed her. The woman said, "Oh my God, why do you kiss me?" The other replied, "I think Jesus told me to." "Oh, no," the woman said, "don't kiss me; it breaks my heart; nobody has kissed me since my mother died." But that loving, sisterly kiss brought her to Christ, and started her on her way to Heaven.

Let love explode in your heart and you will be going out as a witness.

II

THE SECOND MOTIVATION, OR PROPELLING FORCE, IS KNOWLEDGE

This force is our knowledge of God, His Word, and our duty. "To him that knoweth to do good and doeth it not, to him, it is sin" (Jas. 4:17). Let knowledge explode in your heart and mind and you are going to do something, or else end up a miserable, unhappy, chastened Christian.

This force includes our knowledge of sin and what it does.

"We have all sinned and come short of the glory of God." "The wages of sin is death." "The soul that sinneth it shall die." How terrible is the disease of sin. But thank God, we know the cure. Gideon Ouseley, telling of his call to preach, said: "A voice said, 'Gideon, go and preach the gospel.'" But he so felt his ignorance and unworthiness that he pleaded, "Lord, I am a poor ignorant creature. How can I go?" Then it would rush into his mind, "Do you not know the disease?" "Oh, yes, Lord, I do." And the Lord said, "Go then and tell them these two things, the disease and the cure; never mind the rest, the rest is only talk."

This force also includes our knowledge from the Word about Hell. This drives us out. Souls are lost and perishing. Hell is eternal. There is no second chance. We know this from the heart-rending account in Luke 16.

In addition, it includes our knowledge of the second coming of Christ, its imminence, the sureness of His coming. It likewise includes our knowledge of death, its uncertainty but its sureness for all men, if Christ delays His coming.

Our knowledge should drive us out into the

field of service and soul winning. The message ought to burn within us. Our experience should be like that of Jeremiah. "Then I said, I will not make mention of Him, nor speak any more in His name. But His word was in mine heart as a burning fire shut up in my bones, and I was weary with forbearing, and I could not stay" (Jer. 20:9).

III

A Third Explosive Force Which Ought to Send Us Out to Others Is Our Own Salvation

A man who has a genuine case of salvation is going to want to talk about it.

I go to Matthew 10 and the instructions given by Jesus to the twelve. The eighth verse reads, "Heal the sick, cleanse the lepers, raise the dead, cast out devils, freely ye have received, freely give."

Think of what we have received:
Redemption.
A new nature. I'm a child of God.
Forgiveness of sins.
Peace with God and the peace of God.
The privilege of prayer.
Every promise of the Word of God.

Surely we can sing,
"O He's done so much for me,
If I should try through all eternity,
I could never, never tell you what He's done for me."

Now we have freely received, we should freely give. Is it utter selfishness or carelessness which keeps you from telling others about Christ? Do you love the Lord? Do you love lost souls? Do you know God's teachings on sin, death and Hell? Have you been born again?

A true story is given by Dr. Herbert Lockyer of the collision of an excursion steamer with another boat on the river Thames about a half century ago. The boat was crowded with excursionists and the loss of life was great, about 600 perishing in the dark waters. Two ferrymen were called into the coroner's inquest. It appears that these two ferrymen were mooring their boats for the night close at hand, when the crash happened. One heard the crash and the cries, and said, "I am tired, and I am going home; no one will see me in the fog." At the coroner's inquest, the first was asked:

"Did you hear the cries?"

"Yes, sir."

"What did you do?"

"Nothing, sir."

"Are you an Englishman? Aren't you ashamed?"

"Sir, the shame will never leave me till I die."

Of the other the coroner asked:

"What did you do?"

"I jumped into my boat and pulled for the wreck with all my might; I crammed my boat with women and children, and when it was too dangerous to take even one other, I rowed away with the cry, 'O God, for a bigger boat!'"

There are thousands of men and women shipwrecked in the waters of sin, lost and doomed to an eternal death and punishment in Hell.

The Christian who has been gripped by this fact, and who is earnestly trying to save some out of the many, may well cry: "O God, for a bigger boat!" The apostle Paul was having a feeling something like that when he cried, "I could wish that myself were accursed from Christ for my brethren," for they were lost without Christ.

Let us set off for the lost who are drowning in the overwhelming floods of sin, the life saving rocket gun with its story of salvation and its power of redeeming love.

GET WISE TO YOURSELF

"And the Lord commended the unjust steward, because he had done wisely, for the children of this world are in their generation wiser than the children of light" (LUKE 16:8).

Nowhere does the Lord put a premium upon ignorance. Many folks boast about not knowing anything about popular music, or this singer or the other singer. They have an idea they are showing how pious and religious they are.

It may sound pious but not intelligent to say that you never read any book but the Bible. To the contrary the Bible encourages us to be "as wise as serpents and as harmless as doves" (Matt. 10:16).

In our churches we ought to use all the wisdom and initiative we can to carry on. Christ would not condemn different methods of attracting people to the gospel. Some people condemn the use of awards and prizes for children. They say it is wrong and does not do any good. I challenge that statement. If by the offer of some attraction I can get a lost young person to church and under the preaching of the gospel, it is certainly worth while. D. L. Moody built a Sunday School of 1500 in Chicago by handing out a little candy and good things to eat. He won hundreds to Jesus. Yes, be "as wise as serpents and as harmless as doves."

But, now, on the subject, "Get Wise to Yourself," Christ would have you to see yourself as you are. Open your eyes. "Get wise to yourself" is a slang phrase with sound meaning.

I

GET WISE TO THE GAME YOU ARE PLAYING

In this life there are only two sides, right and wrong, good and evil, God and the devil. If your life is aligned with the forces of righteousness, you will win here and hereafter.

If you are playing the game of sin, no matter how smart you may be, you shall lose. No man has ever won in the game of sin. Every man is as an amateur taken in by sharks. The Word says, "Be sure your sin will find you out." Get wise to this matter of sin in your life.

Sin usually finds a man out in this life. Sin has a way of coming to light. Sin sometimes comes out in the lives of others, even in your children. "No man liveth to himself and no man dieth to himself." Get wise to your influence. Which way is it leading?

I spend a lot of time with the children. I love them. God loves them. I have only one fear in my heart, and that is, that I might not always be a good influence for them.

Many parents are careless about their influences. You wouldn't take a million dollars for that boy or that girl of yours, but be careful that your influence is leading them toward Heaven.

What about one of these boys? Robert B. Pattison gives this about the value of a child: A youth is worth $6.50 chemically. He is water and carbon and oxygen and a few other chemical elements.

To his parents his little finger is worth tons of diamonds.

He costs the nation one thousand dollars if he matures righteously, and at least another thousand if he does not.

Christ thought enough of him to die for him.

Sin has a way of coming out; get wise to yourself and to the game you are playing. Watch your influence!

Sin is always found out at the judgment bar. You may think you are winning here but pay day is sure to come. A farmer wrote to the editor of a paper: "Dear Sir: I have been trying an experiment with a field of mine. I plowed it on Sunday. I planted it on Sunday. I reaped it on Sunday. I carted it home on Sunday. What is the result? I have more bushels to the acre in that field than any of my neighbors have had this October."

The editor simply published the letter and wrote beneath it, "God does not always settle His accounts in October."

You can't play in sin and in the game of sin without paying the price. I remember reading of a woman who caught a little creature which she thought was a chameleon, and attached it by a small chain to her collar, so that it could crawl about on her shoulder. The chameleon is a harmless little reptile which changes its color from gray to green or red, and is considered very beautiful by some people. Instead of a chameleon, however, this lady had caught a poisonous kind of lizard, and it bit her, causing her death. What a terrible mistake! And yet there are many who are taking the poison of sin into their lives, thinking it is a beautiful, pleasant thing. But some day they may find they have taken something worse than poison.

II

GET WISE TO THE FOUNDATION OF YOUR LIFE

Are you building upon the sands or upon the rock? In closing the sermon on the mount Jesus described two builders. One built upon the sand and the other upon the rock. One building stood and the other fell.

If you are building upon the sand, destruction is coming. In one of our sea coast towns a large structure was erected. The contractors thought they went down far enough for a good foundation; but after the building was completed, it began to settle. It was built on the sand. It had to be abandoned. Labor, money, material were lost.

Get wise right now! It is sad to find that after building for years, it has all been on the sand.

How many people of advanced age look back with regret to the years wasted. In old age everything crumbled beneath their feet.

Build on the shifting sands of this world and you may expect sorrow. Therefore, build upon the solid rock, Christ Jesus.

III

GET WISE TO THE DIRECTION OF YOUR SOUL

Which way are you headed? You can be headed in only one of two ways, either toward Heaven or toward Hell.

A man without Christ is a man headed in the wrong direction. You may have money, a good home, popularity, power and all the world can give, but without Christ Jesus, you are going the wrong way. You are headed toward a Christless eternity.

Jesus gives us a vivid picture of many people in the parable of the rich fool (Luke 12:16–21).

The rich fool was a successful fool. He had plenty. His ground brought forth bountifully.

He was an egotistical fool. In this story there are seven "I's," five "my's," and a "thou" and a "thine" in the space of three paragraphs. The rich fool left God out of the picture entirely We are all afflicted with this same trouble to a certain extent.

The rich fool was a spiritual fool. Hear his folly: "And I will say to my soul, Soul, thou hast much goods laid up for many years; take thine ease, eat, drink, and be merry."

This man needed to get wise to the direction

of his soul. God said, "Thou fool, this night thy soul shall be required of thee." What does it matter what you have done, and what you have, if in the end you lose your soul in Hell?

Some folks try to ignore the fact of the soul. Some are trying to deceive themselves into thinking they are all right. Others know they are wrong, but keep on putting off the matter of getting right.

Hitler and Tojo are headed in the wrong direction. And so are all the fools who follow Satan. Check on your direction now, before it is too late. Get wise to yourself. Make things right. Repent of your sins, put your faith in Jesus, now!

IS YOUR LIFE A HELL ON EARTH?

"These things I have spoken unto you, that in Me ye might have peace. In the world ye shall have tribulation: but be of good cheer; I have overcome the world" (JOHN 16:33).

All about us we find sorrow, heartache, worry, and trouble. Men's hearts are failing them because of fear. Many are troubled because of the uncertain future. Many are in despair because of the lonely present. Great multitudes are in distress of mind because they are as derelicts upon a stormy sea.

On a few occasions people have made the confession to me, "My life is a Hell on earth." I have talked with some whose nerves had given away. They were suffering the torment of what we commonly call a nervous breakdown.

Ninety nine times out of one hundred the Hell people say they are experiencing is a result of sin; either their own sin or the sin of someone near to them. Ofttimes mothers have suffered great torture of mind and heart because of wayward children. There are wives whose lives are not happy because of lost and sinful husbands.

If the unhappiness of your life is being caused by someone else, you can but pray, trust God, and live consistently for Jesus.

If the Hell you now experience is a result of your own sin and foolishness, resolve now to do something about it.

I want to give you three things to consider:

I

Consider the Hell Endured by Many in This Life

First, let it be understood that this life is never a "flowery bed of ease"; but it need not be one of great unhappiness, either. Christ said, "I am come that ye might have life and that ye might have it more abundantly."

Again, there is peace for all. "Peace I leave with you, My peace I give unto you; not as the world giveth, give I unto you. Let not your heart be troubled, neither let it be afraid" (John 14:27).

There is joy for all. John says, "And these things write we unto you, that your joy may be full" (1 John 1:4).

Yes, abundant life, happiness, joy, peace are yours. Paul wrote, "For all things are yours;

Is Your Life a Hell on Earth?

whether Paul, or Apollos, or Cephas, or the world, or life, or death, or things present, or things to come; all are yours; and ye are Christ's; and Christ is God's" (1 Cor. 3:21-23).

If it is the will of God for man to have all of this, then why all the torment of Hell which is yours?

The Christless life is a Hell on earth. If you are trying to live your life without Jesus, sooner or later great tragedy is coming to you. Perhaps it is upon you now. The emptiness and futility of life is before you. There is no abiding joy or peace outside of Christ.

"To live without Christ is like trying to live without water, for He is the Water of Life.

"To live without Christ is like trying to live without bread, for He is the Bread of Life.

"To live without Christ is like trying to live without light, for He is the Light of the World."

The prayerless life is a life of Hell on earth. Without Christ and without prayer you must carry every burden, every worry, every distressing heartache alone.

Take the privilege of prayer away from the multitudes today and you would fill every asylum in the country twice over in one month. Only prayer is able to strengthen the mothers of this day, only prayer is able to sustain wives whose husbands are in the midst of battle danger. Only prayer can bring the needed strength when the War Department wires, "We regret to announce that so and so is missing in action."

If you have turned away from prayer, come back, remembering, of course, that Jesus is our Intercessor. Trust Him as Saviour, and then "take your burdens to the Lord and leave them there."

The purposeless life is a Hell on earth. The life without a definite purpose and aim is bound to be one of unhappiness. The dawning of the new day holds no enchantment for the drifter. If you have no sure purpose in life, you are a derelict, you are going nowhere, you are accomplishing nothing.

I am afraid that many Christians are miserable because they have no sure purpose in life. They arc not trying to win souls. They are not trying to spread the message of Christ. Their salvation has lost its joy because of selfishness and indifference to the commands of Christ.

If you want to have happiness in life, get something to do and stick to it. It may be merely the teaching of a class of small children.

Put your best into it and joy will come pouring back to you.

The Christless, prayerless, and purposeless life is sure to be a Hell on earth. Many endure it as long as they can and then take the suicide's way out. Others continue to drift on, unhappy and miserable, and making others sad around them.

II

Consider the Hell Which Is to Come

This mental anguish, or physical suffering, you have now is nothing compared to the Hell which is to come for God-despisers and Christ-rejectors.

Some dear people seem to think that all the Hell they will ever have is in this life. But not so! You may have suffered a great deal here, but if you turn your face away from Christ, you are facing an eternity of Hell a million times more intense than anything you have known or imagined in this life.

How terrible are the glimpses Jesus gives of Hell.

"There shall be wailing and gnashing of teeth" (Matt. 13:42).

"And if thy hand offend thee, cut it off: it is better for thee to enter into life maimed, than having two hands to go into hell, into the fire that never shall be quenched: Where their worm dieth not, and the fire is not quenched. And if thy foot offend thee, cut it off; it is better for thee to enter halt into life, than having two feet to be cast into hell, into the fire that never shall be quenched: Where their worm dieth not and the fire is not quenched" (Mark 9:43-46).

Jesus said in Matthew 26:24, "The Son of man goeth as it is written of Him; but woe unto that man by whom the Son of man is betrayed! it had been good for that man if he had not been born."

Jesus was surely thinking of the awful future awaiting His betrayer. If death ended all, then there would have been no reason for such a statement. But death does not end all. Judas is as much alive today as when Jesus spoke. For the centuries to come he will live on in the "second death," which is Hell. "It had been good for that man if he had not been born." Hell is a place of eternal torment. There is no reconciliation of sinners, there is no annihilation of sinners.

III

Consider the Heaven Awaiting All Who Will Receive It

The fulness of Heaven is in the future. A foretaste of Heaven can be had now. "'Tis Heaven below, my Redeemer to know, for He is so precious to me."

There is no greater joy in this life than knowing Christ. He brings Heaven into the heart. He brought Heaven to the despised Zacchaeus. He brought Heaven into the household of Cornelius and the jailer of Philippi.

He took Hell out of the heart of Saul and put Heaven in and said, "Go tell others." He puts a new song in the heart. A young man came to Christ in one of my pastorates, whose heart received the joy of Heaven. He had gone to a picture show on Sunday afternoon and rode out afterward to the church and came in. He was saved that night. After his conversion he couldn't keep still about it. He took a trip from Birmingham to Ohio and at every gas station and restaurant he would tell folks about Christ. He had Heaven in his heart.

But, listen, there's a Heaven to come. No matter how happy you may be here, it's always shattered by sorrow and death, heartache and disappointment. But there is a Heaven to come where this will not be known. Jesus has gone to prepare a place for us. The Son of God knows what to fix up for His followers. The deepest longings of the heart will be satisfied.

There will be complete happiness. Sorrow, pain, tears, separation, and death will be no more (Rev. 21:1–4).

There will be complete knowledge. All mysteries will be explained.

There will be complete recognition. Those loved ones who died in Christ will meet you over there. Friends you said good-bye to long ago will join in singing the song of Moses and the Lamb.

How glorious is the thought of Heaven!

My heavenly home is bright and fair,
No sin nor pain can enter there;
Its glittering towers the world outshine,
Those heavenly mansions shall be mine.

Let Jesus have that old life of yours and see what happens. The hellish unhappiness and dissatisfaction will be replaced with the joy of Heaven, and that is only the beginning.

Is Your Life a Hell on Earth? 79

There is a story told of a famous artist who was falsely accused and unjustly thrown into prison. His jailers allowed him his brush and paints but he had no canvas. The man had not the appearance of a criminal. His sensitive, delicate face spoke of higher things. One day a student of human nature was passing through the prison and seeing the man said to him: "Friend, you do not have the look of a criminal. Why, may I ask, are you here?"

"I am here awaiting trial, but I have been unjustly accused."

"Is there any small service I could do for you?" asked the stranger.

"Yes," said the prisoner, "I am an artist. I would to God I had a sheet of canvas."

The stranger looked about and could find nothing but an old soiled napkin. Pushing it through the bars, he said, "This is the best I can do; see if you can paint a picture upon it."

The artist fastened the napkin to the wall of his cell and began to paint upon it the face of Jesus. He labored upon it faithfully, and every day the touch of his brush brought out more wonderfully the radiant face of the Christ. It later became one of the world's famous paintings of the Master's face and was hung high on a cathedral wall that the reverent gaze of the thousands might fall upon it.

There may be a number of ways that story can be applied, but one seems to be that there is no life so soiled and debased, but that Christ can save it and transform it if He is given the opportunity.

Let Him have your life, and let Him make the "beauty of Jesus" shine out in your life.

ONE WAY HOME

"... *No man cometh to the Father but by Me*" (JOHN 14:6).

More than messages on political reform, more than messages on temperance, more than messages on church discipline, is the need for the message of God's way of salvation.

Thank God, there is a way of salvation, there is a way home, but there is only one way home to God. I remember C. O. Johnson telling about a man who drove into a town and stopped to ask a local boy the way to the Post Office. The boy seemed quite confused, but he began, "Mister, you go down this way three blocks and turn to the right and go one block and turn left . . . No sir, you can't get there that way." He tried again, "Go down this street four blocks and turn right, and go two blocks and then turn left . . . No sir, you can't get there that way." A third time he began, "Go down here six blocks and turn right and go about four blocks and then turn left . . . No sir, I'm sorry, but you just can't get to the Post Office from here."

The world's greatest ignorance is on this

subject: how to get home to God, how to be saved and be sure you are saved.

God has tried to make it simple in His Word, but because of man's sin and depravity, he refuses to receive the simple way. Therefore, we have a multitude of confusing man-made ways of salvation. But, still, there is only "one way home."

There are three reasons why men are so confused.

The devil wants you to be confused and works to that end. Don't forget that the devil is the author of confusion and doubt. He is the "father of lies." The devil wants you to believe a lie and be damned.

False ways are advertised and publicized more than the true way. The writer of a Sunday School quarterly makes the statement, "There are many ways to God." The writer of a column in the Louisville *Times* says, "Nothing is free, not even salvation, for one must be good to be saved." Even in a child's Bible picture book the false ways are advertised; commenting on the story of Lazarus and Dives, it is said, "By and by the rich man died, too. But the angels did not come to carry him to heaven. They paid no attention to him at all because he had not been kind to others while he lived."

Now, let us see the evidence of the Word.

I

BY PICTURE AND TYPE THE OLD TESTAMENT SAYS, "THERE IS ONE WAY HOME TO GOD."

I will give you three or four illustrations.

There was one door to the ark. "And the door of the ark shalt thou set in the side thereof" (Gen. 6:16). This one door was a symbol of the one way of salvation.

The ark was approximately 547 feet long, 91 feet broad, 54 feet high. It had over two acres of floor space. By conservative estimate the ark could carry 5,600 men and provisions. There were only "eight souls" aboard, and the rest of the space was for animals. But with all of its size and space, there was but one door.

The ark was a place of salvation and there was one door in. When they were all in, God shut the door. There is a picture of salvation and security.

There was one way of escape from the death angel when he passed over Egypt (Ex. 12). That was by putting the blood upon the lintel and on the two side posts of the door. The first born of the Egyptians were slain. The Jewish first born lived. "When I see the blood, I will pass over you."

When the tabernacle was built at God's direction, there was one gate to the tabernacle. Again God speaks of the "one way home." This one gate gave the Israelites a means of approach to God. There was no other way.

There was one "altar of sacrifice" in the tabernacle. There was no approach to God save by this altar. There is now but one altar of sacrifice. It is the place where He Himself purged our sins. And in these few examples we are merely touching the evidence of the Old Testament.

II

BY PUNGENT STATEMENTS THE NEW TESTAMENT WRITERS DECLARE, "THERE IS ONE WAY HOME"

Call the roll of the inspired writers; hear Paul in Romans 10:9 ". . . if thou shalt confess with thy mouth the Lord Jesus, and shalt believe in thine heart that God hath raised Him from the dead, thou shalt be saved."

"For by grace are ye saved through faith,

and that not of yourselves; it is the gift of God; not of works, lest any man should boast" (Eph. 2:8, 9).

"This is a faithful saying, and worthy of all acceptation, that Christ Jesus came into the world to save sinners; of whom I am chief" (1 Tim. 1:15).

The writer of Hebrews declares, "Neither by the blood of goats and calves, but by His own blood He entered in once into the holy place, having obtained eternal redemption for us" (9:12).

Hear John as he says, "He that hath the Son hath life; and he that hath not the Son of God hath not life" (1 John 5:12).

Hear Jude: "Now unto Him that is able to keep you from falling, and to present you faultless before the presence of His glory with exceeding joy" (v. 24).

Hear the apostle Peter: "Who His own self bare our sins in His own body on the tree, that we, being dead to sins, should live unto righteousness; by whose stripes ye were healed" (1 Pet. 2:24).

Our whole Bible shouts with a voice of thunder, "One way home." And that is the way of salvation by grace through faith in Christ.

Every other so-called sacred book of the world has one refrain, salvation by works, whether it be the Veda of the Brahmans or the Koran of the Mohammedans. Our Bible is a protest against this from beginning to end.

We believe in good works, but they are the outcome of a grateful heart. Good works are the fruits of our faith.

Other books may have some good teachings and philosophies, but God's Book declares that the way home to God is by Christ Jesus who came into the world to save sinners!

III

By Positive Declaration Jesus Says, "One Way Home" to the Father

"No man cometh unto the Father but by Me." By Jesus we come to our eternal home.

We come by Christ, who said, "I am the door; by Me if any man enter in, he shall be saved, and shall go in and out, and find pasture" (John 10:9).

We come by Christ, who said, "I am the good shepherd; the good shepherd giveth His life for the sheep" (John 10:11).

We come by Christ, who said, "I am the

resurrection and the life, he that believeth in Me, though he were dead, yet shall he live" (John 11:25).

We come by Christ, who said, "I am come a light into the world, that whosoever believeth on Me should not abide in darkness" (John 12:46).

We come by Christ, who said, "I am the way, the truth, and the life: no man cometh unto the Father, but by Me" (John 14:6).

It will avail you nothing to stand and knock at Heaven's door if Jesus is not with you. He alone has the key to admit you to the presence of the Heavenly Father.

Whether rich or poor, educated or ignorant, cultured or crude, Jesus must be your Saviour if you are to come home. Whether you are a drunkard or a total abstainer, whether moral or immoral, whether church member or non-church member, there is only one way home, Jesus. In His first coming He came to prepare us for the place; in His present work in Heaven, He is preparing the place for us; when He comes again, He will take us to the place prepared.

Do you remember the story of John Howard Payne? "Overtaken by misfortune, poverty, and sickness, John Howard Payne went staggering down the streets of Paris toward the garret where he slept. Darkness had fallen. The sleet drove against his face and the cold pierced his thin cloak. Suddenly, a door opened, and the light streamed forth upon the street, the glow and warmth perfuming all the air. Into the arms of the man who stood upon the threshold, happy children leaped, while the beaming mother held forth her babe. In a moment the door closed, the light faded into darkness, and the youth stood again in the sleet and cold, little dreaming that what he was learning in suffering, he was to teach in song. That night, shivering beside his table, the youth lighted his candle, and though the tears fell upon the paper within, like the rain upon the street without, his heart went bounding across the seas, for he knew there was no place like home. He saw the old homestead again, crossed its sacred threshold, saw again the warm smile of the mother long since dead, heard his revered father's voice, heard the voices of dear companions ringing across the green and felt the home that once was behind him was now before him in that Heaven where he should meet again those whom he had loved and lost. And so, with streaming eyes and leaping heart and shining face, he saw the vision splendid and exclaimed, 'There is no place like home,' and sang of home and Heaven.

" 'Mid pleasures and palaces tho we may roam,
Be it ever so humble, there's no place like home;
A charm from the skies seems to hallow us there,
Which seek thro' the world, is ne'er met with
　　elsewhere.' "

Receive Jesus now as your Saviour! He is *the way home.*

THE CHURCH ROLL AND THE LAMB'S BOOK OF LIFE

"And there shall in no wise enter into it anything that defileth, neither whatsoever worketh abomination or maketh a lie; but they which are written in the Lamb's book of life" (Rev. 21:27).

What is a church roll? A church roll holds a record of the names of people presenting themselves for membership and received by the church.

Only saved people are supposed to have membership in a church, but experience and observation teach us that many come and profess eternal life with their lips but do not possess it in their hearts. Consequently, in our churches there are those who profess but do not possess. We know not how many there may be.

What is the Lamb's book of life? The Lamb's book of life is a book containing the names of all who have been saved. This book is God-made and God-kept. When people come repenting of sin and trusting the Saviour, their names are written there.

I

YOUR NAME ON A CHURCH ROLL DOES NOT MEAN IT IS IN THE LAMB'S BOOK OF LIFE

Church membership is not salvation. Conforming to the requirements for church membership will not save the soul. You cannot be a member of many churches without New Testament baptism. But walking forward, answering the pastor's questions correctly, going into the baptistry, and having your name entered upon the roll book will not save your soul.

Many people apparently think that church membership and salvation are synonymous. Again and again people answer my question about their salvation by saying, "I am a member of such and such a church."

Church attendance and church activity are not salvation. I frequently ask the question, "Are you a Christian?" I have had this reply: "Oh, I used to go to church all the time. Why, I never missed a Sunday."

There will be many in eternal torment who went to church Sunday after Sunday. They were faithful in church attendance, but had never been saved.

Let me call your attention to a verse in

Ecclesiastes "I saw the wicked buried, who had come and gone from the place of the holy" (8:10). What a picture that is of those who come and go in our churches and die in their sins. The word "wicked" does not refer only to the killers, thieves, and adulterers. It refers to all who have not accepted Christ.

The inspired writer says, "I saw the wicked buried who had *come* and *gone* from the place of the holy." They had attended the Temple just as the faithful and holy did. They came and they went, and they went as they came, and were buried as wicked persons.

Many come and go from the house of God, because they think that coming and going is all that is needed. They come as lost sinners, they go as lost sinners. And sometimes our churches are to blame: we fail to give them the saving gospel of God.

Some have the habit of coming to church.

Some come out of respectability, but they *go* as they *came*.

Memorizing creeds and rituals will not save. This may not apply to a Baptist church as much as to some others. But it needs to be said.

In some denominations, when a child reaches a certain age, it memorizes a catechism and a

The Church Roll and the Lamb's Book of Life 93

creed of that church. No attention is given to the new birth, nothing is said about an experience of grace.

I am troubled about our own church membership. I fear lest a single one be lost in Hell. But I am more troubled about some of the churches of our land, where the way of salvation is scarcely mentioned. Repentance and faith are never preached. Hell is laughed at. The Bible is discounted.

There is more to salvation than church membership, church attendance, and memorizing the creed and certain verses of Scripture.

A young man kidnapped and brutally killed a little girl in California. He was sentenced to the electric chair. The Associated Press carried the cry of a heartbroken father, and here is what he said: "I can't understand why my son has come to this. I sent him to Sunday School and church when he was little. I told him to read the Bible. I taught him the right ways. Why did he do this?"

There is a whole lot wrong in the statement of that father. "I sent him to Sunday School and church." He should have taken him. "I told him to read the Bible." He should have read it to him. "I taught him the right ways." He did not teach him the Way.

II

Your Name in the Lamb's Book of Life Guarantees Your Salvation

How does it get there? In one way and in one alone. Not by tears, not by the mourners' bench, not by membership, not by living right. It is written there, when by repentance and faith you receive Christ as Saviour.

"But as many as received Him, to them gave He power to become the sons of God, even to them that believe on His name, which were born, not of blood, nor of the will of the flesh, nor of the will of man, but of God."

"To Him give all the prophets witness, that through His name whosoever believeth in Him shall receive remission of sins."

"Jesus saith unto him, I am the way, the truth and the life, no man cometh unto the Father but by Me."

When you do what the Word says, you have the word of Him who cannot lie that your name is written there.

What assurance can we have that our name is written there?

The Word of God assures us. "These things have I written unto you that believe on the name of the Son of God; that ye may know that ye have eternal life" (1 John 5:13). This Word changes not. The witness of the Word of God assures us.

We have assurance by the Spirit. "The Spirit Himself beareth witness with our spirit, that we are the children of God" (Rom. 8:16).

We have the assurance by obedience. "And hereby do we know that we know Him, if we keep His commandments. He that keepeth not His commandments is a liar, and the truth is not in him" (1 John 2:3, 4). If you are not obeying Christ, you have reason to doubt your salvation. This message will make the obedient ones certain of their salvation, but it will make the disobedient ones doubt theirs.

We have assurance by love. "We know that we have passed from death unto life, because we love the brethren. He that loveth not his brother abideth in death" (1 John 3:14).

The Christian loves the company of other Christians and he is not at home in pool rooms and dance halls.

We have assurance by faith. "He that believeth on the Son of God hath the witness in himself" (1 John 5:10). Our faith in Christ is our assurance of salvation. My faith in Christ tells me that my name is written in the Lamb's book of life.

To have your name written there is to be desired above all else. This is the world's greatest honor.

I have seen copies of *Who's Who in America.* It is supposed to be an honor to get your name there. It is greater to have it written in "Who's Who in Heaven."

Jesus, in sending out the seventy disciples, said, "Behold, I give unto you power to tread on serpents and scorpions, and over all the power of the enemy; and nothing shall by any means hurt you. Notwithstanding in this rejoice not, that the spirits are subject unto you; but rather rejoice, because your names are written in heaven" (Luke 10:19, 20).

If you are saved, then rejoice!

If you are not saved, no matter how long you have been a church member, or gone to church, take warning and take the Saviour. There is danger and death in delay. You can go to Hell just as fast from a church roll as if you had never gone inside a church. And I am afraid many are in danger.

My folks live on the Bardstown road at Buechel, Kentucky. My father's property adjoins the Southern Railway tracks. The house is only a few yards, maybe seventy five, from the track. A year or so ago, while my wife and I were visiting at home, one morning my father came in saying a tragic thing had happened on the track near the house. A man in a drunken condition, had gone to sleep between the tracks and the fast passenger train hit him and cut his body into bits. I went out and walked up and down the track and saw evidence of what had happened.

Suppose you had come along there and found the man asleep on the tracks. You looked at your watch and found that it was almost time for the midnight express. What would you have done? You would have pulled him off!

That is the state of every unsaved soul; asleep between the tracks, and God's judgment express is almost due. Receive Christ as your Saviour now! Be sure today that your name is written in the Lamb's book of life.

OUR GOD—A CONSUMING FIRE

"For our God is a consuming fire" (HEB.12:29).

The Word of God gives a number of words to describe the essential character of God. God is Spirit. God is Love. God is light; in Him is no darkness. God is fire; "our God is a consuming fire."

This last solemn, dreadful aspect of God's nature is frequently overlooked. The Lord's nature has not changed. He is still a consuming fire against evil as He declared Himself from Sinai. To the Christian, He is a consuming fire, not to consume us, His children, but to consume all in us which is contrary to His holiness.

To the non-Christian, our God is a consuming fire to judge and punish.

This is a drastic and much needed message for this day. On the authority of this message, I warn you of the judgment of God against sin. I remind you that God loves the sinner and seeks his salvation, but God hates sin.

Let us divide the discussion as follows:

I

GOD CANNOT SANCTION OR APPROVE SIN IN ANY PLACE OR IN ANY INDIVIDUAL

When you sin, remember, God is not on your side.

God always shows His disapproval when His children sin. The Christian in disobedience is sure to feel the consuming fire of God. You are saved, thank God, but you are in for a whipping. "For whom the Lord loveth He chasteneth." Note how God chastens His disobedient children.

He causes the heavens to be as brass. Sin and disobedience in the Christian's life will turn God's ear away from you. "If I regard iniquity in my heart, the Lord will not hear me." Such is the condition of so many today. I meet mothers who are praying for boys in the dangerous battle zones of the world. These same mothers never darken the door of the church. Their lives are examples of disobedience and ingratitude to God. Their prayers do not get higher than their heads.

Peace and joy are taken from you. Your salvation is intact, but because of sin you lose your joy. How many backslidden Baptists have confessed their miserable feelings. I believe that God deliberately takes from you joy and peace to shake you into obedience and godly living.

When all else fails, I believe that God lays His hand heavily upon you, to chasten. God cannot sanction or approve your backslidden condition, therefore the divine fire comes to purify and burn out the dross.

It may be in sickness. (I said "may be" for all sickness is not the chastening of God.) But it may be in sickness. It is wonderful how God can talk to folks when they are flat on their backs. It may be in the loss of position or financial reverse. Your haughtiness and pride must be knocked down. It may be in the loss of some dear loved one. David, a man after God's own heart, sinned a great sin. Because of his sin, Nathan prophesied the death of the child born unto him. The child died.

I conducted a meeting in a college town of Alabama a few years ago. The most active workers of the church were a professor and his wife. I never saw such intense loyalty to Christ and the church. They were soul winners. Their influence was felt in the whole school and the town.

One day I had dinner in the home. They told me of their lives. They told of the precious baby born into their home. They told me of their worship of the child. They quit the church, they robbed God. They lived and planned only for the child. While they were taking graduate work in Peabody College in Nashville, the baby became ill and died in four days. They came home and pondered over the matter. God seemed to point out their sin. They faced it and dedicated their lives to God and His service. Take warning from this. Our God is a consuming fire.

II

THE JUDGMENT OF GOD AGAINST THE WORLD'S WICKEDNESS IS REVEALED IN THIS LIFE

There are many people who think that God ought to be like a compassionate, motherly woman or a grandparent who allows spoiled children to do as they please. However much you may like the idea, the Word, on the contrary, reveals Him as One who hates sin; and One who, when crime demands it, will not hestitate to end the sin by sword or famine or pestilence.

There are often judgments that amaze us. They seem unaccountable. That may be because we have not known what lies behind them. If we could see the conduct of men, as God sees it, we would not be surprised at the afflictions that befall men.

When San Francisco was destroyed, men held up their hands in horror, and said, "Why was such a disaster permitted?" But for a number of years righteous men had been observing the awful trend of the underworld life and saying, "If there is a God in Heaven, that thing cannot be indefinitely continued."

There are various instances in the Old and New Testaments in which God displayed Himself as a consuming fire. Look at the case of Nadab and Abihu in Leviticus 10. This was a deeply solemn occasion. God was dwelling in the midst of His people. God's dwelling place must be holy. Nadab and Abihu did not do according to the command of God, "and there went out fire from the Lord, and devoured them, and they died before the Lord."

Back in the days of Joshua we have another example. A man by the name of Achan disobeyed God and brought into the camp of Israel stolen goods. He paid for his sin with his life.

In New Testament days the fire of God fell to destroy Ananias and Sapphira. They lied to God and immediately they were struck dead.

"Our God is a consuming fire." Those who live in open rebellion to God may feel the judgment of God upon their sins in this life. Men go on in sin and wickedness and rebellion because they think the judgment of God will be delayed.

If I could convince the people of any city that the judgment of God is going to fall upon them, and that before twelve o'clock tomorrow every soul would have to stand before God, you would see the mightiest city-wide revival the world has ever known.

Here is a good illustration from the pages of history. Back in 1721, a Mr. Whitson calculated the return of a comet for the 24th of October at five minutes past five in the morning. He gave public notice of his findings and declared that as a result of the comet's coming the world would be dissolved by fire on the following Sunday.

A great majority of the people believed him. Family prayers were resumed in many homes. Worldliness dropped off. The comet appeared on schedule. The people thought the judgment of God was at hand. Preachers everywhere prayed for the people. Many people burned their novels and rushed to the bookshops to buy Bibles. Men who were living double, sinful lives confessed their sins and sought to make things right.

I don't know how or when God will judge your life or your town, but this I do know, that He will judge sin, and His judgment is often revealed in this life. *The only safe place is in Christ.*

III

Though You Escape Judgment Here—There Is a Judgment Day Coming

"It is appointed unto men once to die and after this the judgment." Every lost soul must stand in the judgment of the Great White Throne. The outcome of this judgment is your just punishment in Hell: the moral, the immoral, the sober, the drunkard, all whose names are not in the Lamb's Book of Life. God will judge the deeds of your life and then will come the awful words, "Depart into everlasting fire."

Flee to Christ today! Receive Him as your Saviour. "But as many as received Him to them gave He power to become the sons of God, even to them that believe on His name: which were born, not of blood, nor of the will of flesh, nor of the will of man, but of God" (John 1: 12, 13).

THE UNIVERSITY OF HARD KNOCKS

"And He said unto me, My grace is sufficient for thee, for My strength is made perfect in weakness. Most gladly therefore will I rather glory in my infirmities that the power of Christ may rest upon me" (II Cor. 12:9).

The University of Hard Knocks is divided into two colleges: the College of Needless Knocks and the College of Needful Knocks. Ralph Parlette traveled the country for many years telling people about the University of Hard Knocks and its two colleges.

There are some needless knocks which we receive. They do us little good and are the result of our own foolishness. Then there are the needful knocks which come to make us what we ought to be.

A grand piano is able to produce good music when touched by artistic fingers because it was knocked and beaten into its present shape. Churches grow by going through the University of Hard Knocks. There must come the hard times to fit us for a proper ministry. Our Sunday School grows by Hard Knocks. Rainy days and grinding work bring success.

Individuals, too, grow by hard knocks.

I

May We Consider Some of the Hard Knocks That Life Hands Out

There is the hard knock of failure. Most of us have felt this hard knock at different degrees of pressure. Some have failed in part and some have failed entirely. The hard knock of failure can either make or break a man.

Sometimes a man gives his best to his work, but advancement is not forthcoming. This hard knock has proved fatal to many. In an Alabama asylum there is a man in a padded cell who failed after eighteen years of what he considered hard work. He served at his job faithfully but others were put ahead of him. He began brooding about his hard knocks and finally his mind cracked.

There is the hard knock of bad health. This is a necessary part of our education for life if we are to sympathize with others. Don't always feel sorry for sick folks. They are learning valuable lessons: the lessons of patience, sympathy, love, faith, and courage. They are going to school.

A few years ago I thrilled at the story of Lou Gehrig, the great Yankee ball player. He played in 2130 consecutive games and then his body failed him. For a long time he had been going down, but he wouldn't give up. In 1938-39 his body failed to respond with the speed and skill of the past. He would fall repeatedly. In the locker room, leaning over to tie his shoes, he would fall to the floor and lie helpless. He never complained to anyone. And then after 2130 games he was forced to drop out. The Mayo Clinic pronounced it infantile paralysis. All of you read of the Lou Gehrig Appreciation Day when 61,000 people turned out in appreciation of Lou. Even with a sick body he tried to work on the City Parole Board in New York. On June 2, 1941, he passed away.

He suffered the hard knock of bad health, and some of you have been through this part of the university.

There is the hard knock of deception, of having your friends betray you. This is one of the hardest knocks a person can have, to discover that a friend in whom he trusted and confided has proved untrue.

A pastor told me that the hardest blow of his whole life was when a trusted friend and fellow

Christian had undermined him. Pretending that he was the pastor's friend, he led the movement to oust him. This is surely hard.

There is the hard knock of persecution. Some of you have had this. The University of Hard Knocks deals out some every now and then. It is hard for us to take the words of Jesus who said, "Blessed are ye, when men shall revile you, and persecute you, and shall say all manner of evil against you falsely, for My sake." Persecution is a part of the consecrated Christian's life.

II

Lessons from Life's Lashings

Since we are going to the University of Hard Knocks every day, we should benefit by this daily instruction. Our difficulties, our heartaches, our failures do three things for us.

They toughen us. They make us able to take it. Most of us are too thin skinned and soft. The hard knocks slow us down too much. A doctor gave me a preparation the other day to toughen the skin on the face and neck. It is to be put on after shaving. It won't kill the whiskers or make it so I won't have to shave again, but it will help to toughen the skin so shaving won't hurt so much.

They teach us. If we are wise, we can learn from the hard knocks. Some folks never learn. But folks who make a success of living have learned from life's University of Hard Knocks. They learn what to do and what not to do.

The failure in business learns what to avoid. A few years ago Mr. R. G. LeTourneau was a complete failure. He was a bankrupt. Today he is one of America's most successful business men, for he learned by his failures.

The person who has suffered from ill health needs to know that God may be grooming him for bigger and better things.

They tender us. Our hearts need to be broken before we can be greatly used of God. Before we can help others we need to be tendered by the hard knocks.

Selfishness, pride, must be knocked out of us. The hard knocks teach us to to be grateful for the good days. The rain and the clouds make us grateful for the sunshine. Our hearts are made tender, so we can sympathize.

III

May We Consider Some Graduates from the University of Hard Knocks

The only fellow who can really help me is the fellow who has gone over the rapids, who has finished a course in this college.

I find a real list of graduates in the Old Testament.

There was a man named Job. Do you remember him? When you think of him, you feel ashamed of every time you have complained about what a hard time you were having. He lost his health, his children, his property. He became an honor graduate of the University of Hard Knocks. But his name stands to inspire men to faith in God down to this day.

There was King David, a man after God's own heart. Surely a favored king such as David didn't have to go to this university. But he did. His life was one of turmoil and persecution. In his young days he was persecuted by Saul, the first king of Israel. In latter years his own family caused him great heartache. His son turned against him, tried to kick his own father out of the kingdom. The boy died a terrible death.

There was Daniel, who graduated with honors from this school. He is known today, almost 2500 years later, as the boy who had the courage to say "No." He was persecuted, hated and despised, cast into a den of lions, and came out with flying colors.

In the New Testament almost every name mentioned is a graduate of the University of Hard Knocks; but there is one who strides out ahead. That one is Paul, the apostle. He was deceived and tricked by his own countrymen. He was whipped and beaten. He was stoned and left for dead. He suffered from ill health, and had to take a doctor along with him. Listen to him, "We are troubled on every side, yet not distressed; we are perplexed, but not in despair; persecuted, but not forsaken; cast down, but not destroyed; always bearing about in the body the dying of the Lord Jesus, that the life of Jesus might be made manifest in our body."

It has been said that since the dawn of history some thirty billions of people have walked this earth. Out of that vast company a scant five thousand are mentioned and remembered today. Who are they? They are the men and women who endured tribulation, labored without reward, suffered without bitterness. They saw the light and were willing to walk in it, and to be blinded by it.

Time does not permit us to list many other honor graduates of the University of Hard Knocks.

John Bunyan was kept in jail by England for twelve years; but instead of giving up, he penned a book which stands next to the Bible.

Oliver Cromwell, during his life, was persecuted and hated; but his name lives.

David Livingstone, born in poverty, worked in a factory when only ten years of age. He labored from six in the morning until late at night, studying his books as he worked. Finally, led of God to Africa, he traveled 29,000 miles on foot, suffered 27 attacks of African fever. His name stands today as one who suffered and endured; he found the grace of God sufficient.

All of these honor graduates of the University of Hard Knocks inspire us to carry on in spite of past failure, ill health, deception, or persecution.

We live in a world of sin, sorrow, sickness, and death. All about us there is pain, heartache, and disappointment, but our God is sufficient. We are going through a school now which will fit us for enjoying the Heaven Jesus has gone to prepare for us.

Use the experiences of life to make you a better man and a better woman. When the going is hard, cling a little harder to God. "His grace is sufficient."

The only thing that remains to be said is that you need Christ, who was tried in all points like as we are, and is able to save, to keep and satisfy. Trust Him today!

SOME THINGS TRUE OF ALL MEN
Acts 17:22-31

There are in the world today 2,120,289,219 people according to the last census, a number so large that few of us can picture it. This number is scattered unevenly over the face of this God-created earth. Eight hundred million people are in China and India alone, 44 per cent of the population of the entire world.

There are five hundred fifty eight million in Europe, one billion in Asia, one hundred thirty one million in Africa.

The world is growing heathen at the rate of six million yearly. In 1935 there were two hundred seventy million more heathen people in the world than in 1890. This is an astounding thing that ought to spur us on to greater mission endeavor.

There are four hundred seventy four million people in China. Four hundred seventy million are not Christian in any sense of the word. Of the four million who make some profession of Christianity, three million are Roman Catholic.

Only 30 per cent of the world's population is enrolled in any church—Protestant, Catholic, or

Jew; 70 per cent, or about 1,564,000,000, are unchurched.

In the United States there are about 130,000,000 people. Of this number only sixty three million are church members. Sixty seven million are untouched by any church.

So much for this brief world picture. Out of this vast number of people in the world, certain things are true of every person, whether he is in the darkest part of Africa or the highest place of culture in this land. It matters not if his color is white, yellow, red, brown, or black, certain things are true of all people.

I

ALL MEN WERE CREATED BY GOD

"And hath made of one blood all nations of men for to dwell on all the face of the earth, and hath determined the times before appointed, and the bounds of their habitations" (Acts 17:26).

God is the creator of all men. Without Him they could not be. Without Him they could not continue to be. Paul makes clear they all came from God. The Athenians claimed to be a special creation. This also struck at the Jewish brethren. Paul affirmed the unity of the human race with a common origin and with God as Creator.

II

All Men Are Naturally Religious

That does not mean that all men worship the one God, Jehovah. Many worship the material of the world created by God—the sun, moon, river, storm, trees—but fail to see God.

The Athenians were religious people, far more religious than most of us are. The American Standard Version says, "I perceive that in all things you are very religious, for as I passed by, I saw your gods" (Acts 17:22). In verse 16, Paul saw a city full of idols. Some 30,000 gods cluttered up the town of Athens.

All men seem naturally religious. They worship something or other. It is not just religion that men need. It is more than that. The Africans, the Chinese, are religious, but they need Christ.

III

All Men Seek a Common Goal in This Life

The goal of men is peace, happiness, security,

contentment. This means freedom from sickness, sorrow, pain, as much as possible. This means achievement, for achievement brings happiness. This means recognition, because the struggle of the masses of mankind is for recognition in life.

Some seek to reach the goal through power. So they try to build themselves into power.

Some think life's goal can be attained through the acquisition of wealth. On the road to wealth men soon find that it takes more than money to make a living.

It takes more than money to make a home.

It takes more than money to make a man rich.

It takes more than money to heal a broken heart.

It take more than money to stifle an enraged conscience.

Some think that all of life can be realized through the pursuit of knowledge.

Another strives to reach the goal by shutting out the world.

Others strive to reach the goal by plunging into all of life and drinking of every fountain.

The ambitious man drives himself at his work and hopes to realize.

The lazy hobo seeks the rainbow's end through the line of least resistance.

Some seek the goal through Christ and service to Him.

It is said that while seeking the best out of life many get the worst. "Beauty turns to ashes."

The majority of men seek the goal on the wrong road.

IV

All Men Desire an After-life

There may be a question in the mind about it, but there is a deep desire for it. The Indian of the western plains believes in Heaven. So does the man of Africa and Asia.

"If a man die shall he live again?" This life in no way satisfies man. He desires immortality. Every man will reply at once, "I want to go to Heaven."

From the Hottentot of Africa to the penthouse dweller of New York, there is a desire of man to live on.

V

All Men Are Sinners

Sin is contrary to the nature and person of

God. Sin is a slap in the face of God. No man can plead not guilty before God.

All are proved to be under sin. "What then? are we better than they? No, in no wise: for we have before proved both Jew and Gentiles, that they are all under sin; As it is written, There is none righteous, no, not one" (Rom. 3:9, 10).

" . . . ye walked according to the course of this world . . . fulfilling the desires of the flesh and of the mind; and were by nature the children of wrath, even as others" (Eph. 2:2-3).

All have gone out of the way. "They are all gone out of the way, they are together become unprofitable; there is none that doeth good, no not one" (Rom. 3:12).

"All we like sheep have gone astray; we have turned everyone to his own way; and the Lord hath laid on Him the iniquity of us all" (Isa. 53:6).

We are all guilty before God. "For whosoever shall keep the whole law, and yet offend in one point, he is guilty of all" (Jas. 2:10).

All men have come short. "For all have sinned, and come short of the glory of God" (Rom. 3:23).

So it is proved by the Word of God that all men are sinners.

VI

All Men Are Lost

"The soul that sinneth it shall die"; "Wherefore, as by one man sin entered into the world, and death by sin, and so death passed upon all men, for that all have sinned" (Ezek. 18:20; Rom. 5:12).

How we fight against such preaching; sinners, lost and condemned. We get mad that anyone should say such a thing to us. I am not saying it; the Word speaks.

VII

Praise God!—All Men May Have Salvation in Christ

All are sinners. Sin brings death. This is a sad picture. But God *so* loved that He gave. In Christ Jesus we have salvation and eternal life. "God is no respecter of persons." Jew and Gentile, white, black, yellow, red, or brown may have salvation in Him.

The invitation is "Come." "And whosoever

will, let him take the water of life freely" (Rev. 22:17).

"Neither is there salvation in any other; for there is none other name under heaven given among men, whereby we must be saved" (Acts 4:12).

Yes, in Christ there is salvation and peace for all men, who will come to Him.

John R. Rice told how a friend of his in Chicago, who had lived a life of sin and shame, was converted one night in a mission.

After he was saved he brought his old mother to Chicago to live with him. When she would go down in the mission and an opportunity would be given to quote Scripture, she would always quote, "Yea, though I walk through the valley of the shadow of death, I will fear no evil, for Thou art with me."

But there came a time when his mother was no longer able to attend the mission, and he knew her time was short. One day the doctor who had charge of the case said to him, "If you have anything to say to her, you had better do it now, for she can't last much longer."

He went over to her bed and said, "Mother, do you know the condition you are in?" She answered, "Yes, son, I know I'll never get well."

He said, "Mother, I have heard you talk so many times about Jesus being with you in the valley; how is it now?" She answered, "I never felt His presence more in all my life."

Again he said, "Mother, I want to put it to a test, and I am going to ask you from time to time if He is with you. I want you to let me know by a word or a look, and when you step into the boat and start across the river, if Jesus is with you then, I want you to press my hand."

Presently he bent over her and asked, "How is it now?" and she said, "Each moment He grows sweeter than He ever was before."

The physician came over and held her pulse; her son got on his knees and took her hand in his. His wife knelt on the other side of the bed and held the other hand. The moments fled swiftly by, then the doctor whispered, "She's gone."

When he did, the wife, with tears streaming down her cheeks, said, "Husband, she is pressing my hand." And he answered, "Yes, thank God, and she is pressing mine."

You need Jesus in life and in death. Take Him now.

FACE TO FACE

"For now we see through a glass, darkly: but then face to face; now I know in part; but then shall I know even as also I am known" (1 COR. 13:12).

There are two kinds of mirrors on the market today, plate glass and window glass. One gives a clear reflection, the other not so clear.

Ancient mirrors were of polished metal, not glass, and far from perfect. But no matter what kind of mirror, the reflection is quite different from looking at the person, being face to face.

Paul is saying that now we see everything in a mystery. We see in part, we know in part. We do not fully see and know. How true that is. How mysterious are many things of life; not complete mysteries, for we do know in part, but puzzling to us in our imperfect state.

May I start your thoughts upon the matter.

I

THE PROBLEM AND MYSTERY OF WAR

Men cannot fully understand the why of war

and bloodshed. The Word of God gives an explanation, but even that we do not understand fully, for we see and know in part.

Some are asking the question, "Why doesn't God stop war?"

Perhaps it is because God respects man's freedom. God created man a free moral agent. He could have made him differently. But if man was merely a machine, every action of which was controlled by God, then there would be no sin, suffering, love, sorrow, or hatred except by the moving of the hand of God upon the machine. I believe that God respects man's freedom. Man has the power of choice.

God does not stop war because in this age in His dealings with men, His activity is not that of public judgment, but of redemptive love and grace.

Perhaps He does not stop war and sin in general because He desires man's love and not simply his fear. Yes, there is a certain reverential fear which man should have of God, but I am thinking of fear much lower than that.

Someone asks, "Why doesn't God stop Hitler? Why doesn't He smite him and put him out of the way?" My friend, would you be willing for God to deal with you and your sins on the same basis? When through your eyes you are guilty of lustful thinking, would you like God to strike you blind on the spot? When you lie, would you have God paralyze your tongue so that you could never speak a falsehood again?

God does not wink at sin, but He is not dealing with men on that basis now. There is coming a day of judgment for all. Now we see and know in part, but one day, face to face.

II

THE MYSTERY OF SUFFERING AND AFFLICTION

Here is a good saint of God who suffers in nameless ways. He lives in constant pain. Why must this be?

Charles H. Spurgeon suffered much pain of body. His suffering was so intense that for two or three months each year he had to be out of his pulpit.

The great Paul suffered much. He besought the Lord to take away the thorn in the flesh until the Lord gave His answer, "My grace is sufficient for thee."

Yes, many of the world's great Christians and great people bore and do bear much bodily pain and suffering and affliction. Yet it seems that God has a plan in it. At least God helps men to use their afflictions to do great things. Someone said, "The school of adversity has more noble graduates than any other university in the world."

Milton, the poet, was blind; Beethoven, the musician, was deaf; yet

> To blind old Milton's rayless orbs
> A light divine is given:
> And dear Beethoven hears the hymns
> And harmonies of Heaven.

The mystery of suffering is with us, but ofttimes suffering and affliction have been used to the glory of God and the uplift of mankind.

Some day the mystery shall be done away and we shall know.

III

The Mystery of Death

In the very prime of life a useful and good person is taken from this life. We cannot understand. Why should it be the children, or young, vigorous folks, when some aged, suffering one remains?

IV

The Mystery of Poverty and Failure

A good person fails in spite of all efforts and intentions while an evil one prospers. For the average person there is a puzzle. A day of judgment comes for the wicked, but now the mystery. The mystery of iniquity doth work.

Some people beat their heads and cry, "I cannot understand. God is not fair."

Notice again. "Now we know in part and we prophesy in part." "Now we see through a glass darkly." But one day, "when that which is perfect is come, then that which is in part shall be done away."

But one day we shall see face to face! But one day we shall know even as God knows us!

But now, what shall we do?

Search the Scriptures and pray for a better understanding of God's will and way for this world and for us. To close the Bible, as some do, would be like turning off the light in your room and praying for light, when you need to push the button. In the hour of greatest darkness, search the Bible and pray for the light of God upon your path.

Trust God.

Submit yourself completely to His will and trust Him fully. You cannot see the whole way ahead of you; only a part. Ask for light upon the one step and trust Him fully.

Lead, kindly Light, amid th'encircling gloom,
   Lead Thou me on,
The night is dark, and I am far from home;
   Lead Thou me on,
Keep Thou my feet; I do not ask to see
   The distant scene;
One step enough for me.
Look to that "land that is fairer than day," when complete knowledge and understanding and sight shall be ours.

Not now, but in the coming years,
   It shall be in a better land,
We'll read the meaning of our tears,
   And there, sometime, we'll understand.

We'll catch the broken thread again,
   And finish what we here began;
Heaven will the mysteries explain,
   And then, Ah then, we'll understand.

Why what we long for most of all,

Eludes so oft our eager hand;
Why hopes are crushed and castles fall,
　Up there, sometime we'll understand.

God knows the way, He holds the key,
　He guides us with unerring hand;
Sometime with tearless eyes we'll see,
　Yes there, up there, we'll understand.

Then trust in God through all thy days,
　Fear not for He doth hold thy hand,
Tho' dark thy way, still sing and praise,
　Sometime, sometime, we'll understand.

Lost man, you say there is much you do not understand, but there is much you can understand. You can understand the awfulness of sin. All about you are the evidences of sin and the devil. You can feel your own need of salvation, seeing your lost condition, feeling convinced of sin.

Even a child can understand God's way of salvation.

"The soul that sinneth it shall die." But God sent His Son, "who took upon Him the form of a servant and was made in the likeness of men; and being found in fashion as a man, He humbled

Himself, and became obedient unto death, even the death of the cross" (Phil. 2:7, 8).

"But God commendeth His love toward us in that while we were ye sinners Christ died for us" (Rom. 5:8). The sweetest mystery in all the world is the mystery of God's love for sinners.

"For the wages of sin is death but the gift of God is eternal life through Jesus Christ our Lord" (Rom. 6:23).

"Verily, verily, I say unto you, he that believeth on Me hath everlasting life" (John 6:47).

> One day we shall see His face
> With all the saints above,
> And sing forever of His grace,
> Forever of His love.

A woman who had lost her health in following the gaieties of the fashionable world was reclining on her bed, longing for the society and pleasure that she had once enjoyed. She told her nurse to fetch the box that held her jewels, so that she might amuse herself in recalling to her memory the festive seasons when she had worn them to the admiration of many.

"Now, nurse," said she, "would you not like to have some of these jewels?"

"No, ma'am, not at all, for I have jewels much finer."

"How can that be, nurse? Mine are the finest jewels in the land. Where are yours? You never wear them."

The nurse held up her Bible, saying, "My jewels are in here!"

The lady, thinking that there were some hidden away in the Book, said, "Take them out and show them to me."

"Why, ma'am, my jewels are so precious, I only show you one at a time."

Then she opened her Bible and read, "I have learned in whatsoever state I am, therewith to be content" (Phil. 4:11).

She told her of the treasure that she had in Heaven; how that, though poor, she had a loving Father, who provided for her, and the great happiness that she had in Him, and how she was patiently waiting for the Kingdom to come.

"Why, nurse, I never heard anything like that; how happy you must be to feel as you do! I wish I could do the same."

The next day the woman said, "Nurse, I should like to see another of your jewels; the one you showed me was so beautiful."

The nurse again opened her Bible and read, "This is a faithful saying, and worthy of all acceptation that Christ Jesus came into the world to save sinners" (1 Tim. 1:15).

From the few words that followed, the woman's heart was opened to feel that she was a sinner, that Christ Jesus was her Saviour; and she soon found rest, peace, joy, in believing and trusting Christ Jesus as her Saviour.

Out of the pain of suffering, this one was led to Christ, to know in part the mystery of His love and grace which only in Heaven we shall fully understand. So thousands learn anew each day, that while now we see through a glass darkly, then shall we know even as also we are known.

THE PURPLE HEART

"But He was wounded for our transgressions, He was bruised for our iniquities; the chastisement of our peace was upon Him; and with His stripes we are healed" (ISA. 53:5).

I have been attracted by the frequent notices in the papers when men have been decorated with the Purple Heart. I understood something of the meaning of this decoration and I sought to know more of what it meant.

This medal is presented only to men who are wounded in action. I have read the history of the medal. It was first established by General George Washington, on August 7, 1782. It was revived by the War Department on February 22, 1932, out of respect to the memory and military achievements of Washington.

On the face of the medal is a relief bust of George Washington in the uniform of a General of the Continental Army. On the reverse side appears the inscription for "Military Merit," with the owner's name beneath.

There are three things suggested by the possession of this decoration.

1. Sacrifice

2. Suffering

3. Shed Blood

We shall honor everyone who sacrifices and suffers and sheds blood in the defense of our country and our liberties. We shall honor those who bear scars received in the thick of the battle. There may be some patronizing persons who will scoff at war-won medals. Such a one needs to be reminded of the words of Shakespeare who said, "He jests at scars that never felt a wound."

But after thinking thus briefly of those who suffer, sacrifice, and shed blood in the defense of our country and our liberties, it is easy to turn to speak of One who came to this world almost 2000 years ago—He who came to wage a one man war against sin and Satan. He came not to live but to die. He came not to save His life but to lose it.

Of Him the Word says, "He was wounded for our transgressions, He was bruised for our iniquities . . ."

When this war is over, we will thrill to the stories of bravery, suffering, and death. But after all is said, the greatest death of this world was the death of Jesus. Great men have died in the history of the world. But never one so great as the Son of God. Men have died for great causes. But none so great as the cause of Christ. Men have died to defend their homes and loved ones. Christ died to save even His enemies.

There are three things I want to point out about the death of Jesus. Don't ever forget them.

I

THE DEATH OF CHRIST WAS VOLUNTARY

"As the Father knoweth Me, even so know I the Father; . . . Therefore doth My Father love Me, because I lay down My life, that I might take it again. No man taketh it from Me, but I lay it down of Myself. I have power to lay it down, and I have power to take it again" (John 10:15, 17, 18).

Christ came to this earth of His own free will to die. He was sent of the Father, to be sure. However, He did not come to die under force. He came as a lamb to the slaughter. Christ did not die because the devil and his forces were stronger than He. Christ died because He wanted to die. It was His choice to die. It was for the purpose of dying that He came forth from the Father.

"Therefore doth My Father love Me, because I lay down My life."

II

The Death of Christ Was Victorious

His disciples might have imagined that He failed. His mother and brothers and sisters might have thought He failed, but never was won a greater victory.

I have read again and again the words, "It is finished" (John 19:30). They are words of victory. The victory of Christ was the victory of completion.

When you die, you will leave a thousand jobs unfinished. Christ finished His task. He finished the bridge from sinful man to sinless God. He built the highway over which man can come to God. "The way of the Cross leads home, there is no other way but this."

I read in a magazine of the completion of the military highway to Alaska. If there had not been war on, we would have had some kind of nationwide celebration. One of these days you can get in your car here in the States and drive to the heart of Alaska. Christ, too, has completed a road, a way to the heart of God.

Think of it another way. In the victorious death of Christ on the cross He pierced the darkness of man's sin and brought light and salvation to men. Think of it again. The death of Jesus completed a way for men to escape death, destruction, and Hell.

I shall never forget the Louisville flood of 1937. I drove my car in the highlands helping in every way I could. And then I helped my father and many other men in the building of a pontoon bridge. We built frames, placed barrels inside of them, and as they were finished, pushed down upper Jefferson Street. Finally it touched some of the buildings where people were trapped by the flood waters and they began to walk back over the bridge to safety. The bridge carried small, big, rich, poor, young and old, in fact everyone who would trust himself to it, that he might not be beaten and vanquished by the flood waters.

Jesus has provided a way of escape from the flood waters of sin. The words of Jesus, "It is finished," were words of victory. He conquered sin, death, and the grave (1 Cor. 15). But there is one more word describing the death of Jesus.

III

THE DEATH OF CHRIST WAS VICARIOUS, SUBSTITUTIONARY

"But God commendeth His love toward us, in that, while we were yet sinners, Christ died for us"; "who His own self bare our sins in His own body on the tree, that we, being dead to sins should live unto righteousness; by whose stripes ye were healed"; "For I delivered unto you first of all that which I also received, how that Christ died for our sins according to the scriptures" (Rom. 5:8; 1 Pet. 2:24; 1 Cor. 15:3).

Someone asked Charles Haddon Spurgeon when he was in his last illness if he could state his faith in one sentence, and without a moment's hesitation, he said, "Jesus died for me." How true! Christ died for our sins.

The story is told of a woman who stopped by the bedside of a dying boy in a hospital in London. The boy was as much as heathen as if he had been born in Central Africa. Guided by the Spirit she told him the story of Jesus, and then said, "Sonny, God made you; God loves you; God came down from Heaven and died for you; and now He is going to take you home to be with Him forever." He said,

"Say it again, lady." She said it again twice over: "Sonny, God made you; God loves you; God came down from Heaven and died for you; and now He is going to take you home to be with Him forever." Pulling himself up by the rope hanging over the bed, the boy, who seemed to have gained new vitality, said, "Lady, thank Him for me." But before she could respond, he fell back lifeless, and went home to thank God face to face.

Is it possible in a short sentence to present our faith? Absolutely. Here it is: "Christ died for our sins." The death of Christ was vicarious. He died in our place. The death I deserved He died. He bore my sins. He took my penalty.

I read of an incident which occurred many years ago. A company of soldiers were rebelling against their officers and commanders. They were finally brought again into submission and obedience. A severe punishment was decided on for the offenders. The men were ordered to line up in one long line and then commanded to count off by tens. Every tenth man was ordered to step forward and was taken away to die. In that line were a father and son. They were standing next to each other. The father looked straight ahead. The boy watched the counting. He heard the count come down the line. He noted that his father was to be a tenth man. The counting was coming fast—5, 6, 7, 8, 9—he quickly shoved his father aside and shouted 10, and marched away to death.

We were all under the count of ten, but "Christ died for our sins." Through His sacrifice, suffering and shed blood, we may have pardon and victory.

BY THE RIVERS OF BABYLON

"By the rivers of Babylon, there we sat down, yea, we wept, when we remembered Zion. We hanged our harps upon the willows in the midst thereof" (PSA. 137:1,2)

This verse takes us back to the captivity of the Jews in Babylon. Psalm 137 was written in reminiscence of that day of the children of Israel. The words picture their sadness and their dilemma in a strange land.

Back of the captivity was their sin of disobedience. They had failed to heed the warnings of Moses given in the Book of Deuteronomy. When firmly fixed in the Promised Land they turned from Jehovah to worship other gods. Moses foretold what would happen when they forgot God. It happened; captivity came. They were carried by the thousands into Babylon to be slaves of the Babylonians. Jews are not the kind of folks to be slaves even though much of their history comes from their years of bondage in Egypt and Babylon.

Their lot in Babylon proved to be a hard one and memory added to their burdens. So the Psalmist declared, "By the rivers of Babylon, there we sat down, yea, we wept, when we remembered Zion."

By the rivers of Babylon they sat down and talked about Jerusalem and cried. They thought of former blessings enjoyed back in the Promised Land and cried like children. They remembered their freedom to come and go as they pleased. They remembered the Temple in Jerusalem. They remembered their festival times and the happy days of fellowship. They remembered how their cousins, uncles, and aunts came from Nazareth and Bethlehem up to Jerusalem for the special days. Precious memories came flooding in and the tears came. Tears of memory; I have seen them many times, tears of memory over lost blessings. Do you cry sometimes, friend, when you remember how things used to be in your life?

I

FOR SOME OF YOU THE JOY OF SERVICE IS GONE

You once got great joy out of serving Christ, but that joy is gone now and you are doing nothing. Every city is full of folks who used to be active church workers. Back in the old home town or village where they came from, they were active, but now they do nothing.

The world, the flesh, and the devil kept crowding in: a craving for money; a desire to get ahead in life. All of it took you from your place in the service of Christ. Some of you were active soul winners at one time. What joy belongs to the soul winner! But now, you are doing nothing. The joy you once had in serving Christ is gone.

Listen, friend, opportunities are going by. Many of them will never come again. There is an old saying, "The mill will never grind with the water that is past." Sitting on the sidelines, you are losing daily opportunities to serve Christ and your fellowman. By the river of Babylon you sit and weep over lost blessings.

II

For Others the Joy of Song Is Gone

The Israelites wept by the rivers of Babylon and hanged their harps on the willows. Their captors came out and said, "Sing for us! Sing us a song of Jerusalem." But they said, "How shall we sing the Lord's song in a strange land?" They could not sing the songs of the Lord in a heathen land. They were heart-sick over lost blessings. Their sin and servitude were an embarrassment to them. The joy of song was gone.

Backslider friend, how can you sing when your heart is not right with God? You have been saved and you know it, but you are out of the center of His will. You can't sing the Lord's song. You might sing the devil's song, but not the Lord's.

Try singing the Lord's songs in some of the places to which you have been going. Try singing "My Jesus, I Love Thee," or "All to Jesus I Surrender" in some of the devil's places. It can't be done. Lot couldn't sing the Lord's song down in Sodom. He was in the wrong place and his conduct was all wrong. When he tried to testify, his kinsfolk laughed at him.

David couldn't sing the Lord's song when he fell into the devil's trap. Abraham couldn't sing the Lord's song when he got down in Egypt and began telling lies about his wife.

Try singing the song of the Lord when your heart and mind dwell in strange lands. The heart that holds to sin, any sin, silences the Lord's song.

God loves music. It is one of His best gifts to man. He put that marvelous mechanism in the human throat and lungs; an endowment of forty four muscles capable of 173,000,000 variations of sound. God wants us to sing His song as a testimony. If you can't sing with the lips, you can have a song in your heart. What is the Lord's song? It's the song of Jesus and His love.

Biederwolf tells of a man who had no song. A minister went to see a man who was very ill. He asked him about his soul.

"Well," the man said, "I think my chances for getting to Heaven are pretty good."

"Do you believe there is a Heaven?"

"Yes."

"Do you believe there is a Hell?"

"Yes, there must be."

"Do you believe your soul is immortal and will soon be forever in one or the other of these two places?"

"Yes," he answered earnestly.

"Well, you must have a reason for thinking your chances for Heaven are pretty good; would you tell me what it is?"

The answer came slowly as the man said, "Well, I've always been a moral man and respectable; I've been kind to my wife and children, and I have not intentionally wronged anyone."

"That is very commendable; but what kind of place do you think Heaven is?"

"I think it is a very happy place, without sin or sorrow, and I think they sing a great deal there."

"Yes, you are right; and do you know the song they sing?"

"No, I have never thought about that."

"Well," said the minister, "I will read it to you."

And turning to Revelation 1:5, he read, "Unto Him that loved us and washed us from our sins in His own blood; to Him be glory and dominion forever and ever."

"You see," said the minister, "they are praising their Saviour, the One who loved them and died for them. They haven't a word to say about what they have done; it's all about what He has done. He loved them and He died for them. Now, suppose you get to Heaven in the way you say—because you have been good to your family and so on. There would be one sinner in Heaven who couldn't join in the song they sing; you would be there without a Saviour and you would have no song to sing."

And as if waking out of a dream, the man said, "I had never thought of it that way before!"

He then became extremely anxious about his soul and wanted to have the question settled at once.

Turning to 1 Timothy 1:15, the minister read, "This is a faithful saying and worthy of all acceptation, that Christ Jesus came into the world to save sinners, of whom I am chief." And the man said: "That's me; and I want to accept Him now."

He lived but a few days, but when the minister came back the man said, with a strange new light of joy in his face, "I'll have a song now. It will be unto Him that loved me and washed me from my sins in His own blood."

He fell into a peaceful sleep, and in a few moments was gone to join the heavenly choir and sing the song that only the redeemed can sing.

Lost friend, don't you want the Lord's song?

Christian, has the joy of song left you? Then come back to God.

III

For Some People the Joy of Salvation Is Gone

This sums up everything. You will have to

think carefully; not salvation gone, but the joy of salvation gone. The Word teaches that your soul is secure when once entrusted to the Master. The joy of salvation depends upon our attitude, activity, and consecration. Too many professing Christians are sitting now by the rivers of Babylon and weeping because the joy of salvation is gone.

Two young women confessed to me after a church service that once they had been saved, but now all joy was gone. They had not attended church in some time. They had not prayed regularly. The Holy Spirit made them miserable in the service, showing them where they were. Salvation was not gone, but joy was.

I received a letter sometime ago from a friend of recent years, a deacon, a superintendent of Sunday School, a soul winner, a Bible scholar—but the old devil had crept in. His letter was four pages long, with one cry: "I'm away from God, pray for me."

Three things usually contribute to a loss of joy.

Absenting yourself from God's House. No man can keep spiritually aglow and neglect God's House and public worship.

Neglect of spiritual activity. Neglect of the

Word of God, neglect of prayer, indifference toward the spiritual welfare of others, cause us to lose our joy.

Some special sin or sins. How many Christians have lost the joy of salvation by taking to themselves some sin, or by failing to conquer their besetting sin!

If you are not having the joy in your Christian life you ought to have, something is wrong. Are you weeping over lost blessings? "O for the joy that once I knew when first I knew the Lord."

But, friend, don't sit there weeping. Do what God tells you. Repent of your wrong, confess it to Him, pray for His forgiveness. Get up and get out of the strange land.

You have His promise. Take it. Your desire to get back to God is an evidence that you were once there. You can't go back to a place where you have never been. If you once knew salvation, its joy, its service, and its song, then come back.

King David shows us the way back. He was God's man, but he fell into awful sin. The devil laid a bear trap for him and caught him off guard. When God pointed His finger at him through the prophet Nathan, David acknowledged his sin and cried for forgiveness. Psalm 51 gives the steps a man may take to come back into fellowship with God, and Psalm 32 tells of complete forgiveness. It is probable that Psalm 32 was written after Psalm 51. Notice Psalm 32:5. "I acknowledge my sin unto Thee, and mine iniquity have I not hid. I said, I will confess my transgressions unto the Lord; and Thou forgavest the iniquity of my sins."

If you have failed in church attendance, Bible study, prayer, soul winning; or if some sin has crept into your life, confess it to God. Come forward for the reconsecration of your life. Come out of the strange land; come into God's promised land.

One thing ought to constrain many to come forward. It is the sacrificial death of Christ. The loving, sacrificial death of Christ constrains me, as a Christian, to give my best. It ought to bring all of you backsliders back to the Lord. The death of Christ for lost sinners ought to touch your hard hearts and bring you forward in acceptance of Him. He died for you.

Those men and boys in the distant battlefields have my heartfelt thanks. Most of them are giving themselves willingly for what they think is a righteous cause: to make our world peaceful and safe, at least for a few years. Because they are fighting and dying for me, I would gladly shine the shoes of any one of them.

No doubt somewhere last night, some mother's son made the supreme sacrifice. His plane rode high and proud in the sky, but now it is just a twisted pile of wreckage. "The fine head and the shining face and the broad shoulders remain only a picture that looks out upon a quiet living room on a shaded street an eternity away.

"Last night in those agonizing hours of unspeakable isolation, he went through a thousand deaths without the one thing that might have helped a little, the sound of a familiar voice, the touch of a friendly hand. Many people died last night in their beds at home, surrounded by those who cared. Last night he died in utter desolation, in unimaginable loneliness.

"The pain was terrible enough. But then there had to be that dreadful burden of thought in those endless last hours. Mom and Pop. The flowers blooming again in the back yard. The good old roadster in the driveway. The last sweetheart kiss at the station. The half finished letter in his blouse. All those plans for the future. Buddies back at the field, 500 miles across the water, wondering. Couldn't somebody find him, please? The wracking pain again."*

That digs down in your heart, doesn't it? Certainly the price they are paying is great, and very few appreciate it as they should. Oh, but think tonight of the price paid for your salvation. The death of God's Son on Calvary's tree! Let it break your heart. Surrender to Him now!

Sing with the hosts of the redeemed, not a lament for lost things, but the song of deliverance. Weep no more in a strange land where sin has taken you, but return to Christ that your joy may be full as it was in the days of old.

---
* From the Louisville *Courier Journal*.

RESCUED BY ANGELS

In Genesis 13 Abraham and Lot parted company. Lot chose the beautiful, well watered plains of the Jordan and went to live in the sinful city of Sodom. Abraham dwelt in the land of Canaan.

In Genesis 14 Lot was captured by Chedorlaomer and Abraham went to his rescue.

In Genesis 18 Abraham prayed his great intercessory prayer in behalf of the city of Sodom.

In Genesis 19 the cities of Sodom and Gomorrah were destroyed by fire and brimstone, but Lot was rescued by angels.

I

THERE CAME TWO ANGELS TO SODOM

What a contrast! Two heavenly beings in the midst of the sin and wickedness of Sodom; they came, conscious of the iniquities all about them. What agony of soul for heavenly ones.

Sodom typifies to us our present world reeking in sin. The whole present world system is sickening to the child of God. The open sin of America is disgusting to the average Christian, let alone to the Lord Jesus. Think of it:

Seven billion dollars spent each year for liquor.

Five hundred thousand dispensaries.

Over one million barmaids.

Fifteen billion dollars spent for crime each year.

One out of every one hundred girls of marriageable age a prostitute. Thirty five years ago the average age of fallen women was twenty three; today it is sixteen and seventeen.

Somebody murdered every forty five minutes in the United States.

Between twenty and twenty five thousand suicides each year.

Eighty five million Americans attend the movies each week.

The gambling business takes seven billion dollars a year.

One out of every five marriages ends in divorce.

What does the Lord Jesus Christ think of America? Over half of the people of this land make no profession of faith. Only ten per cent or less of the people of America ever go to church on Sunday morning. Only a fraction of one per cent of professing Christians engage in soul winning. Only one per cent out of every American dollar finds its way into the church treasury. Almost twenty five cents out of every dollar goes for luxuries.

Almost two thousand years ago Christ came into this sin-cursed world. How the sin and filth must have grated upon His divine sensibilities! But He did not come to inaugurate social reform. He came, the sinless One, to die for the sinful.

He did not come to clean up the foul smelling evils of the Roman government. He came as a Lamb to the slaughter, to die for the redemption of all who would believe on His name. That was His first coming.

He is coming again one of these days. First, into the atmosphere above us to catch up the saints. Then, to come down upon this earth to put down sin, chain Satan, and establish His kingdom.

"Yes, there came two angels to Sodom."

II

They Came from the Lord

These angels were not self-appointed ambassadors, they came because God sent them.

They had a definite commission from God. They realized the work was not theirs, but God's. They had come in His name, and in His strength to do His will.

Every preacher, every teacher, every gospel singer, and every soul winner is going to grow weary if he does not have the assurance that God has sent him. When you know you are God's servant and in God's place for you, you can carry on for Him.

Many a time I might have quit were it not for the knowledge that I am God's messenger. I grow tired of arguing, fault-finding, backbiting. I grow tired of the foolish mechanics forced upon us these days. I grow tired of the indifference of this lost world. I grow tired of the luke-warm condition of Christians and churches. I grow sick of our hypocrisy. But I know that God has called me, I must try to bring His message. I try to make my message the message of the Lord. For that reason, I don't stand around to receive criticism of my messages. My wife doesn't do so. My deacons don't do so. I try to make my message from the Lord.

The angels were sent from God, and they said, "The Lord has sent us." When our blessed Christ came, He said, "As the Father has sent Me, even so send I you."

III

They Came with a Message from God

God sent the angels to Lot with a threefold message.

The angels brought a message of salvation; "Up, get you out of this place." Salvation was offered to Lot and his family. The city was going to be destroyed, but God's missionaries came to save Lot.

An even more glorious message of salvation was brought to us by Christ. He came with the good news. He brought us the message of God's love and willingness to forgive. He came to fill out for us the picture of a loving God, a forgiving God.

I was moved by an illustration from the *Sunday School Times*. A wealthy business man in Boston, a devout Christian, married a woman and gave her a beautiful home. She fell, through the besetting sin of drink. One day she left home, never to return, leaving a note behind her saying that her life was not in keeping with her husband's sterling Christian character. He immediately employed men throughout the land to search for her. Copies of her photograph were left in various cities with undertakers, with these instructions: "If her body should ever come to you, buy the finest clothes that money can buy, give her the finest casket possible, bank it with flowers, and send for me." When at last an undertaker called him and he gazed upon the face in the casket, through his tears he said, "Oh, Nellie, if you only knew how I loved you, you would have come back to me." When the funeral was over, he went to the marble works and contracted for a costly monument. When asked what should be inscribed on it, he said, "I want you to engrave on it just one word, *Forgiven*."

Oh, the glorious message of love and forgiveness! You can have your money and your houses and lands, but give me the joy of sins forgiven! Give me the joy of knowing God's love in my heart.

The angels brought a message of judgment. "For we will destroy this place, because the cry of them is waxen great before the face of the Lord; and the Lord has sent us to destroy it."

God could no longer stand the awful sin of Sodom. The angels were sent to tell of His coming judgment. And truly when Lot went out, which is a picture of the rapture, fire and brimstone rained down upon the city and destroyed them all.

Our present world is hastening toward a similar judgment. God is long-suffering, but when sin and wickedness reach a certain place, then God will step in with judgment.

The first universal judgment was in the time of the flood, when the world system that then was, was destroyed by water. The second universal judgment will be during the Great Tribulation. The third judgment will be at the Great White Throne. Then will come the period of which Peter wrote in the Spirit: "The elements shall melt with fervent heat, the earth also and the works that are therein shall be burned up."

O sinner friend, the God of love, who in mercy calls you to Him, will one day be the God of wrath and judgment.

The angels brought a message of great urgency. The angels came and gave their message of salvation and judgment. But Lot, who typifies many people of this day, hesitated, lingered, procrastinated. Doubtless he did not want to leave his home and his goods, his friends and his business. How like many of us.

Lot had much in Sodom, but he had to lose it. My friends, why do we cling so hard to the material things of life? Lost men remain lost because their eyes can see only the goods of this world.

Christians are kept from victory and real service because of selfishness and greed of worldly things. Suppose someone would offer you the possession of a great palace for one day, or the possession of a cottage for a hundred years: which would you take? Why, the cottage, of course. Remember, the child of God is an heir of eternal things. He possesses them right now.

But notice Lot. "And while he lingered, the men laid hold upon his hand, and upon the hand of his wife and upon the hand of his two daughters, the Lord being merciful unto Him. And they brought him forth, and set him without the city" (Gen. 19:16).

There is a whole sermon in that verse.

Lot lingering.

Two urgent personal workers—the angels.

The Lord being merciful unto him. Lot did not deserve all of this personal attention of God and angels, but God was being merciful, just as He is being with you.

These angels of the Lord saw the coming danger. They saw "the wrath to come," therefore they acted with urgency.

This whole story is a picture of your condition and need, lost man. God has given His message to you. We are trying to warn you of danger. We want to press home the need of repentance and faith *now*. Christ, who is higher than angels, is calling for you.

We seek to persuade you as the angels persuaded Lot to leave Sodom. We would not have your blood upon our hands.

Dr. George Truett tells of the funeral of a sixteen year old girl which he was asked to conduct. Seeking information that would help him in his ministry of comfort, he was told by the mother, "Dr. Truett, she was our only child."

"Yes, but you sorrow not as others that have no hope," said the preacher.

The mother answered, "That is where the trouble is; we have no such hope. Our daughter was not a Christian."

The mother wept bitterly while she continued, "While it is true that her father and I were both members of the church even before she was born, it is also true that our darling girl lying in that casket never heard either of us pray. She was not converted, and we fear that she is lost and her blood will be upon us." Then she became hysterical at the thought of a lost daughter.

Relating the incident later, Dr. Truett asked: "Who would dare say that her blood would not be upon them?"

Be reconciled to God before it is too late. Hear the message of the angels, of salvation, of judgment and of urgency, and, like Lot, be rescued, by these warnings, from the wrath of God, and enter into the kingdom of the Son of His love.

YOUR FORTUNE TOLD—FREE

I have no message on fortune telling. Most people know the teaching of the Word of God and need no further instruction. I have never been to a fortune teller and I never intend to go to one. When fortune tellers live in million dollar pink palaces and drive Cadillac automobiles and have servants waiting on them hand and foot and give $500,000 to charity each year, then I am going to see them. But as long as they live in cheap trailers and rent dirty rooms in cheap buildings, they can't tell me a thing. I feel like saying, "Physician, heal thyself." The whole world will honor the man who succeeds, but does not have time to waste with the man who is always telling the other fellow how to succeed.

I don't propose to have my fortune and future told from tea leaves, coffee grounds, or the palm of my hand. I am not going to waste my time watching someone look at a crystal ball and guess about my past, present, and future. I know about my past, and my present. My future is in the hands of God. The only time I got near to having my "fortune told" was on a weighing machine. I put in a penny and a card dropped out which read, "210 pounds. Better watch your weight, sister."

But I can give the fortune and future of every person who reads this message. It is very simple, for there are but two classes of people in the world: Christians and non-Christians, sinners saved by grace and sinners lost.

I

LET US TAKE FIRST THE PAST OF ALL MEN

Four words describe the pitiful plight of all people until Jesus takes over.

You were *helpless*, without life and without strength. "You were dead in trespasses and sins," spiritually dead to God, and buried in graves of your own making, in "trespasses and sins." You walked according to the course of this world. You were carried away by the current of the world's influences and like a dead fish in the stream, were without any power of resistance.

You were *hopeless*, "having no hope" (Eph. 2:12). How miserable is a man's condition when he is without hope! How dark the day when no ray of hope shines in! It is hope that keeps a man smiling when death is clutching at his heart.

> Have Hope! It is the brightest star
>   That lights life's pathway down:
> A richer, purer gem than decks
>   An Eastern monarch's crown.
> The Midas that may turn to joy
>   The grief-fount of the soul;
> That paints the prize and bids thee press
>   With fervor to the goal.
>
> Have Hope! As the tossed mariner
>   Upon the wild sea driven
> With rapture hails the polar star—
>   His guiding light to haven—
> So Hope shall gladden thee, and guide
>   Along life's stormy road,
> And as a sacred beacon stand
>   To point thee to thy God.

The past of men without Christ is hopeless.

You were *homeless*. Without Christ a man is homeless. ". . . at that time ye were without Christ, being aliens from the commonwealth of Israel, and strangers from the covenants of promise . . ." (Eph. 2:12). We are all pilgrims but we are not homeless if we have Christ.

In this day many people are homeless. In the war-torn countries, hundreds of thousands wander from place to place without a home. Hitler has made thousands homeless. I read of a family in Germany driven from a home of long standing, mother, father, daughter, and little son. The Gestapo came and demanded all the valuables in the home. When the small son did not obey as they wished, he was beaten over the head with the butt of a revolver. When he put his hands on his head to ward off the blows, the butt of the pistol broke every finger. Finally, the family was driven from their home and left to wander the countryside, the father carrying the broken body of the little son.

Without Christ, my dear friend, you are just as homeless. You are like the prodigal son sitting in the hog pen.

You were *godless*. You were godless in a world teeming with evidences of His wisdom and power. In the world, loved by God, where God's own Son lived, loved and died to save sinners, you were without God. You say, "But I have always believed in God." If you did not believe in God's Son, the Word of God says you were godless (Eph. 2:12).

Yes, that is the picture of every believer

before he came to Christ. Your past was one of sin and darkness, "but God . . ." And that is the picture of every lost person's past, helpless, hopeless, homeless, and godless.

II

But Now See the Present

We must see first, the present of the Christian.
Save for the gracious love of God we would all still be helpless, hopeless, homeless, and godless. "But God, . . . is rich in mercy."

Because of His grace we are alive in Christ. "And you hath He quickened, who were dead in trespasses and sins." The Holy Spirit of God has breathed into you the breath of a new life. A man does not begin to live until Jesus comes in.

We are reconciled to God. "And that He might reconcile both unto God in one body by the cross, having slain the enmity thereby" (Eph. 2:16). Sin separates from God, but in Christ we are made at one with the Father.

We are members of the household of God. "Now therefore ye are no more strangers and foreigners, but fellowcitizens with the saints, and of the household of God" (Eph. 2:19). We are the sons of God. "To as many as received

Him to them gave He power to become the sons of God." We are heirs of God and joint-heirs with Jesus Christ. Because we are sons we have the privileges of sons. We have access to the presence of God. We have the promise of God's help. We have the promise of His protection.

We must also see the present of the unsaved. If you are unsaved, your condition, my friend, is unchanged. What you were in the past you still are.

You are condemned. "He that believeth on Him is not condemned; but He that believeth not is condemned already, because He hath not believed in the name of the only begotten Son of God" (John 3:18).

You are under the wrath of God. "He that believeth on the Son hath everlasting life; and he that believeth not the Son shall not see life; but the wrath of God abideth on him" (John 3:36).

You are in bondage. "Whosoever committeth sin is the servant of sin" (John 8:34). You are bound by chains that will not break. Your mind, body, and soul are under the power of Satan. It is told of a famous blacksmith of medieval times that, having been taken prisoner and hid away in a dungeon, he began to examine the chain that bound him, in the hope that he could find a flaw in it where it might be broken. But soon he discovered it was a chain of his own make; and he had often boasted that no one could break the chains he made. Even so men are forging chains that shall bind themselves, and chains that cannot be broken. Every evil word, and deed, and thought, strengthens the links until nothing but the coming of Christ, the Great Deliverer, can rescue them, and set them free.

III

Your Future

The past of every person is one of darkness and sin. The present for many of you has been changed by God's love. Now, what about the future? This is the question people are asking today. Most people are too much concerned about the days *just* ahead of us. We should be concerned, but our greatest concern must be over our eternal future. "Where will you spend eternity?" is the question God is asking you today.

God, who knows everything, and by whom

everything was made, has revealed His purposes and plans to men. He would have you know that there are only two places created for man's eternal future. One is Heaven, and the other is Hell. You are asking "How can I know where I'll spend eternity?" I can tell you exactly, if you will answer truthfully one question: "What have you done with Jesus?" Is He your Saviour or not?

If Christ is your Saviour, you are as sure of Heaven as if you were there right now. That is the Word of God "who cannot lie." Your future is as glorious as the promises of God, for they are all yours.

You are going to the City of God. Back in Revelation 21, 22 you have a description of the Holy City. It is 1500 miles long and 1500 miles wide. If it were placed on the North American continent, the cornerstone would be laid on the Pacific coast at the boundary between Canada and the United States. Then the wall would proceed eastward across British Columbia, Alberta, Saskatchewan, Manitoba and into Ontario as far as Lake Superior. Then southward until it reached the Gulf of Mexico; from here west to the Pacific coast. Conceive of all that territory forming one big city.

The city is built upon twelve foundations, each being a massive, precious stone. The jasper walls will be 216 feet high. In each of the four walls there will be three gates, each composed of a single pearl. Towering above all this will rise the city of God for 1500 miles, 400,000 stories high.

Inside the city the streets will be paved with the purest gold. There will be the Tree of Life and the River of the Water of Life. The saints of all the ages will walk up and down the avenues. There will be no lighting problems for the Lamb is the light thereof. There will be no housing difficulties for in the Father's house are many mansions. There will be no money problems, for the very streets are paved with gold. There will be no unemployment, for all will be serving Him. There will be no tears, no sorrow, and no death, no graves on the hillsides of glory.

I'm bound for that beautiful city,
   The Lord has prepared for His own,
Where all the redeemed of all ages,
   Sing glory around the white throne.

Sometimes I grow homesick for heaven

And the glories I there shall behold,
What a joy that will be when my Saviour I see
In that beautiful city of gold.

If Christ is not your Saviour, you are as sure of Hell as if you were there, unless right now you take Jesus.

Ah, you say, "Isn't there some other way?" There is no other way. Christ is the only Saviour, and Hell is the future portion of all out of Christ.

Hell is the abode of Christ-rejectors. Whether good or bad, moral or immoral, church members or non-church members, Hell is the place for men out of Christ.

Hell is an eternal place. There is no escape. There is no release. There is no annihilation.

Hell is a place of eternal torment and suffering. So said Jesus Himself. The loving Son of God proclaimed the awfulness of eternal fire.

But, thank God, there is hope for you. You need not be lost unless your will is set against God. You can be saved today. Christ died to save your soul!

Suppose that I held in my hand two records tonight. One is a record of righteousness, purity, honesty, virtue, good deeds, patience, mercy and sacrifice. This world has seen only one record like that. Not a mark of sin mars its perfection. The other record is one of sin, unrighteousness, imperfections, evil passions, broken promises, dishonesties, evil thoughts and evil words.

One is the record of Christ, the other is your record and mine. They hang side by side, but now Christ comes and writes His name at the top of that shameful list of sin, and writes our name over that long record of glorious things. Under our guilt he goes to the cross, and to death and to the grave. Under His name we can approach Heaven. We are given eternal life. We are given His righteousness. That is the message of redemption in Jesus. He died for you and me.

When a young girl was brought to the Saviour, she memorized the verse, Isaiah 53:5, "But He was wounded for our transgressions, He was bruised for our iniquities; the chastisement of our peace was upon Him; and with His stripes we are healed." Often she repeated it, because her life, previous to her belief in Christ, had been very sinful.

Just a few minutes before her death, while her loved ones were standing about her bed, she raised her weak hand to her brow and softly said, "There are no thorn-pricks there, because He was wounded for my transgressions." Then with the finger of her right hand she felt the palm of her left hand, and with fading breath, said, "There is no nail-print there, because He was wounded for my transgressions." Then slowly she placed her hand on her side and faintly said, "There is no spear-print there, because He was wounded for my transgressions; He was bruised for my iniquities; the chastisement of my peace was upon Him . . ." With a smile of confidence she closed her eyes.

No, we need no fortune tellers to reveal our past, present or future. Christ has taken care of the past. He is our present Saviour. He has graven every believer upon the palms of His hands (Isa. 49:16). There is our fortune and there is our future, in His keeping.

DANGER—DEADLY POISON

"Wherefore seeing we also are compassed with so great a cloud of witnesses, let us lay aside every weight and the sin which doth so easily beset us, and let us run with patience the race that is set before us" (HEB. 12:1).

With every person there is some sin to which he is especially prone. This might be called his besetting sin. There are three classes of folks with regard to besetting sins. Some know their besetting sin, but do nothing about it. Some know their besetting sin and are battling to conquer and cast it out. Others have won the battle over their besetting sin.

Your besetting sin is the sin that "so easily besets you." It clings to you, it wraps itself around you like a cloak, it fastens itself to you like a parasite. It is like the gray moss on a Florida tree. It is dangerous to the life. Therefore we must get rid of that besetting sin.

I hold in my hand a bottle of poison. This is about as deadly a poison as can be found. There are eight teaspoonfuls in this bottle. The contents of this single bottle, by chemical analysis, is sufficient to kill one hundred thirty persons. I want to get rid of this poison. I don't want it around. It is dangerous, it is deadly. I wouldn't think of unscrewing the cap and putting it to my lips.

Just as I do not want this deadly poison to pass my lips and go into my body, so I do not want to harbor known sin in my life.

What is your besetting sin? It will differ in almost every life.

It might be temper, or an evil tongue; love of money, or covetousness; false pride or jealousy. It might be an unforgiving spirit; it might be envy; it might be self-seeking, selfishness; it might be gossip.

It might be fault-finding; it might be laziness. By prayer, by self-examination, we must know what it is and seek to be free from it. This besetting sin is dangerous and deadly.

Your besetting sin is the sin you do not want to be reproved for; the sin you are readiest to defend; the sin your thoughts run most upon; the sin you find the most excuse for; the sin that often beclouds your spiritual sky; the sin that causes remorse of conscience the most frequently; the sin that makes you doubt your present acceptance with God; the sin you are most unwilling to acknowledge you possess;

the sin that you are most unwilling to give up; the sin you are all the time trying to persuade yourself is an infirmity.

It is for you to admit and confess to yourself what is your besetting sin.

Why must we so earnestly seek to be free from this besetting sin?

I

BECAUSE IT WILL DULL SPIRITUAL PERCEPTION

Sin accounts for the dullness, spiritually, of the great masses of Christian people. They are dull of hearing. They are not spiritually alert.

The mother of John and Charles Wesley once said to her boys, "Whatever weakens your reason, impairs the tenderness of your conscience, obscures your sense of God, or takes off the relish of spiritual things, in short, whatever increases the strength and authority of your body over your mind, that thing is sin to you, however innocent it may be in itself."

Sin destroys our love for going to the house of God. Sin clouds the pages of the Book. You want to read the Bible and understand, but its meaning remains a mystery. The reason is sin. Sin closes the door to prayer. You may go through all the form of prayer, but it is meaningless.

I want to be a wide awake Christian. I want to read the Word of God and feel that the Spirit is unfolding its meaning to me. I want to pray and know that God is hearing and will answer.

That besetting sin, whatever it is, will dull your spiritual perception. Get rid of it. Confess it to God and ask His help to overcome.

II

It Will Defeat Victorious Christian Living

I am talking to Christians now. Your soul is saved and safe in Him. Every Christian wants to live a victorious Christian life. To be victorious you must oust that besetting sin.

That besetting sin will defeat you in your quest for *peace*. Your conscience and the Holy Spirit will hold it up before you. Peace in your heart cannot be complete until things are made right. You may have a perfect pair of shoes, but one small tack will destroy all comfort and joy of wearing them. One besetting sin, though it seems small, will take away peace from your heart.

That besetting sin will defeat you in your quest for *power*. We all desire to have spiritual power. We are ashamed of our powerlessness. We want power to live, testify, and win souls.

That besetting sin will hinder you in your *progress*. We desire to grow in grace and in the knowledge of the Lord and Saviour. That sin, which clings like a parasite, will hold us back. If we want to run the Christian race and win, we must lay aside the weight and the sin which easily besets us.

Christian friend, what shall we do about this matter? We must obey the Scriptures.

"If we confess our sins, He is faithful and just to forgive us our sins, and to cleanse us from all unrighteousness." With David we must come and say, "Lord, I acknowledge my transgressions; and my sin is ever before me."

Whatever it may be, get rid of it. Begin now to conquer it in Jesus' name that you might have peace, power, and progress in your Christian life. Otherwise, it will dull your spiritual perception, it will defeat victorious Christian living.

I have a word to say to the lost man about his besetting sin. What will your besetting sin do for you?

III

It Will Damn Your Soul

The chief sin of the lost person is unbelief. Some of you are saying, "Preacher, you don't know me. My worst sin is drink." "My worst sin is hatred." "My worst sin is worldliness."

All of that is bad, but can be changed when you believe on Jesus. The sin that God sees against you now is the sin of unbelief. The worst sin is the sin of unbelief, rejection of Christ.

Would you care to drink from this bottle of poison I hold in my hand? No, of course not. But when you reject Christ, you are doing a more deadly thing than drinking poison. Rejection damns the soul forever. Rejection is the devil's poison to put you in Hell. "He that believeth not is condemned already."

Sin is a deadly poison, the effect of which may not be felt today, but it never fails in its deadly work. The only antidote for the poison of sin is the salvation of Christ.

Someone has said,

"Columbus could discover a new world; Jesus alone could discover man's deepest needs. The Wright brothers could perfect an airplane; only Jesus could perfect the plan of salvation.

"Fulton could invent a steam engine; no one

but God could invent the scheme of redemption.

"Edison will be remembered by the incandescent light; Christ will be remembered as the light of the world.

"Wilberforce and Lincoln will go down in history as emancipators of races; Jesus alone will go down in history as the Saviour of races from sin.

"All who have ever lived and died could not save one soul; Christ's death is sufficient to save every soul."

When Lincoln had been assassinated and the body was being carried home for burial, in Albany, New York, a Negro mother stood on a street corner, and, lifting her child above the heads of the people, pointed to the casket and said, "Look, honey, look! that man died for you."

I point you to the Lamb of God who takes away the sin of the world. He died for you.

Sin is poison.

Sin is deadly.

Sin is eternal death.

The only escape for any man is by the way of the cross. Take Jesus now as your Saviour. "Believe on the Lord Jesus Christ and thou shalt be saved."

THE BIBLE—THE COMPASS OF LIFE

"Wherewithal shall a young man cleanse his way? By taking heed thereto according to Thy word.

With my whole heart have I sought Thee: O let me not wander from Thy commandments.

Thy word have I hid in mine heart, that I might not sin against Thee.

Blessed art Thou, O Lord. Teach me Thy statutes.

With my lips have I declared all the judgments of Thy mouth.

I have rejoiced in the way of Thy testimonies, as much as in all riches.

I will meditate in Thy precepts, and have respect unto Thy ways.

I will delight myself in Thy statutes: I will not forget Thy word" (Psa. 119:9–16).

No one can overestimate the greatness and worth of the Bible. I believe that one of the great dangers in the average person's life is that he will come to consider the Bible as just a book, a book which every home should have, but one never referred to. The Bible must be read, believed and practiced.

John Wesley said, "I am a Bible-bigot. I

follow it in all things, both great and small."

George Washington said, "The world cannot be governed without this Book."

John Quincy Adams said, "The first and almost the only Book deserving of univesal attention is the Bible."

Abraham Lincoln said, "In regard to the great Book, I have only to say that it is the best Book which God has given to men."

Another danger in many Christian lives is that they will put the Bible aside saying that they cannot understand it. Spurgeon used to tell the story of an old man who said, "For a long period I puzzled myself about the difficulties of the Scripture, until at last I came to the resolution that reading the Bible was like eating fish. When I find a difficulty I lay it aside, and call it a bone. Why should I choke on the bone, when there is so much nutritious meat for me? Some day, perhaps, I may find that even the bone may afford me nourishment."

Let us consider the Bible briefly in four aspects.

I

It Is Food for Weary, Tired Travelers

This world can never satisfy the spiritual

hunger of the soul. When you are weary and tired, sitting down with the Word is like sitting down to a satisfying meal, or drinking a glass of cool water when you are thirsty.

In a very spiritual service some time ago, and listening to a message right out of the Word, I heard someone whispering back of me. It has always annoyed me when folks talk in church when I want to hear the speaker and when they ought to be listening. But I turned my attention from the speaker to hear the voice back of me. As I listened I noted that the person back of me was whispering the Scripture right after the speaker. No matter what he quoted, this dear woman quoted right after him. And then I heard her whisper, "Amen. Isn't that glorious?" I glanced around at her and saw that she was a white haired woman of seventy or more. Her face was radiant, her eyes were fastened on the speaker, and she was drinking in every word. She didn't know that she was whispering, but she was feeding on the Word. She was like a weary, hungry traveler drinking in the Word.

II

THE BIBLE IS A BOOK OF ETERNAL COMFORT FOR THE SAD AND TROUBLED

In this time of great trouble and sadness many people are putting themselves to sleep at night with the comforting words of the Lord ringing in their ears.

"The Lord is my shepherd, I shall not want."

"Let not your heart be troubled, ye believe in God, believe also in Me."

"And we know that all things work together for good to them that love God, to them that are the called according to His purpose."

In time of death the Bible is our source Book for comfort. In normal times 50,000 people die every day; 2083 every hour, 34 every minute. Every time you breathe some soul is going out into eternity. The hush of death is over the world. Only God can comfort our hearts, and He uses the Word of God to speak to you.

In time of separation from dear loved ones the Bible will comfort and cheer our hearts. I am not overly emotional, but I shed tears in railroad stations while waiting for my train and noticing the sad partings: wives and husbands saying good-bye, not sure they will ever see each other again; fathers saying good-bye to their children.

Standing near me in the line waiting to get on a train in Cincinnati was a negro sailor, his wife, and a boy of some eight or nine. The negro sailor was crying, his wife was crying, the boy was crying, and the negro father knelt down and looked into his boy's face and said, "Son, don't forget your daddy. Remember, I'll be thinking about you every day."

I watched an old father, mother, and two sisters say good-bye to a brother in the station at Detroit. After the boy had gotten on the train, they turned to one side and the four of them cried with great heaving sobs. If they know Jesus, and if they know the Word, they can stand the separation, for if we never meet again here, we shall meet up there.

III

THE BIBLE IS A GUIDE FOR STUMBLING, FALTERING MAN

"Thy word is a lamp unto my feet, and light unto my path."

When I went into the lobby of the Statler Hotel in Detroit some time ago, I saw an unusual thing. About one third of the lobby was taken up with a large platform and all sorts of shining machinery, but in the center of the whole display was a large red metal cylinder about four feet high and about two feet in diameter. This red affair was weaving from side to side. This was the Sperry Gyro-Compass, built by Chrysler, for the ships of the United States. The rolling and tossing of the compass was done to illustrate the rolling of the deck of a ship, and to show the accuracy of the Sperry Gyro-Compass.

The Sperry Gyro-Compass is made of 10,000 individual pieces. It weighs 600 pounds. It is said to be one of the most intricate and delicate instruments devised by man. Once this compass is set to point accurately to north and south, no magnetic force or natural cause can affect it. The old magnetic compasses are useless because of German magnetic mines, but this compass is always right on the line. It is built to an accuracy never known before. It is said to be the most precise instrument ever conceived.

No matter how the ship rolls and tosses, the compass stays pointing to the true north. I said to myself, "That is marvelous, but the

Christian has an even better guide for his life."
He has two, the Holy Spirit and the Word of
God. The Word of God is our compass through
the stormy seas of life.

> Lamp of our feet, whereby we trace
>   Our path when wont to stray.
> Stream from the fount of heavenly grace,
>   Brook by the traveller's way!
>
> Bread of our souls, whereon we feed,
>   True manna from on high!
> Our guide and chart, wherein we read
>   Of realms beyond the sky.

All questions of life and conduct are answered
in this Book. The Bible is your guide Book in
business. It is your guide, your compass, in
social life. It is your guide in home life.

IV

THE BIBLE IS A LOOKING GLASS IN WHICH MAN CAN SEE HIMSELF AS GOD SEES HIM

The Bible picture of man is always true. It is
not flattering. I read in a magazine of a large
and expensive beauty shop where the lights and
mirrors were so arranged as to make almost any

woman look like a beauty. The lights and mirrors eliminated the wrinkles, the skin blemishes, and other defects, and women were greatly flattered with their appearances.

The Bible doesn't doctor your appearance. It reveals you as you are. The Bible looks you squarely in the eye and says, "You are a sinner." You may say, "Oh, I'm not so bad." The Bible answers back, "You are a sinner, and if you say you have not sinned, you make God a liar." We have all sinned and come short of the glory of God. "There is none righteous, no not one."

The Bible looks you squarely in the eye and says, "You are lost and on the road to Hell." Some men are offended when the preacher says that, but you let the Word speak to your heart now. Get a picture of yourself and your condition. "The soul that sinneth, it shall die." "The wages of sin is death."

The Bible looks you squarely in the eye and says, "You have only one way to be saved." That way is in Christ. You can't argue with the Word of God. Listen to it, my friend; it is the voice of God Himself speaking to you. Here is what it says: "You are going to die, for it is appointed unto men once to die."

Here is what it says: "You have to stand before God. For every one of us must give an account of himself to God."

Here is what it says: "Prepare to meet thy God."

Repent and believe, chart your course by this Book and you will come to safe harbor.

700 B. C.
Isaiah 53

Many times I have witnessed feats of magic and marveled at the dexterity of the fingers and ability of a trained magician to fool an audience. I have been amazed, and yet I know that there was a human explanation for it all.

I saw a man drive a car blindfolded through the streets of a little Kentucky town one day. I was amazed, but I knew that there was some human explanation.

I recently heard Dunninger over a national hook-up. Dunninger demonstrates each week his ability to read minds. What he does is uncanny and amazing, but I'm sure there is some human and natural explanation.

But there are some things that amaze which cannot be explained in human and natural terms. The prophecies of the coming of Christ fall in this category.

Seven hundred years before He was born an inspired writer gave a complete prophecy of the suffering Saviour.

In 700 B. C., it was written, "He is despised and rejected of men." Seven hundred years later an inspired writer said, "He came unto His own and His own received Him not."

In 700 B. C., it was written, "with His stripes we are healed." Seven hundred years later a Roman governor named Pilate, who knew nothing of God's Word or prophecy, had Jesus whipped and delivered Him to be crucified.

In 700 B. C., it was written, "He opened not His mouth; He is brought as a lamb to the slaughter, and as a sheep before his shearers is dumb, so He openeth not His mouth." Seven hundred years later we read that when Jesus was being tried "He answered him never a word, insomuch that the governor marvelled" (Matt. 27:12).

In 700 B. C., it was prophesied, "He made His grave with the wicked, and with the rich in His death." Seven hundred years later it was so. Read John's record.

In 700 B. C., it was written, "And He was numbered with the transgressors." Seven hundred years later He was led to Calvary's hill and "there they crucified Him, and the malefactors, one on the right hand and the other on the left." He was numbered with the transgressors; count the crosses, one, two, three.

This prophecy of 700 B. C. tells us about three things.

I

Our Sin

Verse 6 "All we like sheep have gone astray; we have turned every one to his own way; and the Lord hath laid on Him the iniquity of us all" (Isa. 53:6).

The inspired writer left nothing to the imagination. "Our transgressions . . . our iniquities . . . we have gone astray . . . we have turned every one to his own way."

The greatest tragedy in this world is sin. It was sin that nailed Christ to the cross. We are not bewailing the fact that Jesus died, but we are troubled about the sin that made it necessary for Him to die. Sin nailed Him to the cross, your sin and mine.

The Word tells us "we have all sinned and come short of the glory of God."

How hard it is to get a man to see himself a sinner. How hard to get him to say, "I have sinned." How hard to get people to see themselves as lost. "The soul that sinneth it shall die." "The wages of sin is death." Right now is the time to realize these truths, not hereafter in Hell.

II

HIS SUFFERINGS

Our sin made necessary His sufferings. How the Word seeks to picture the sufferings of Jesus. Listen: "He was wounded . . . He was bruised . . . He was chastised—whipped with stripes . . . He was oppressed . . . He was afflicted . . . He was made an offering for sin."

Every Christian ought to take account of the suffering Saviour. Before you pass on down the road of indifference, before you enter into the worldliness that will bring shame to Christ, consider the suffering Saviour.

Before you absent yourself from God's house, consider the suffering Saviour. A preacher put out as publicity, "One thousand vote against evening service." The church had 1300 members, the average attendance on Sunday evening was 300, therefore 1000 of the members were literally voting against the service.

Every lost man ought to pause before the suffering Saviour. Before you shrug your shoulders and go on down the road to Hell, consider the Christ who suffered and bled and died for you. That you might be saved He allowed men to wound Him, bruise Him, whip Him, spit on Him, slap His face.

He is your sin bearer, "who His own self bare our sins in His own body on the tree, that we, being dead to sins, should live unto righteousness; by whose stripes ye were healed.

III

Our Salvation

The Word makes clear our sin, the Saviour's sufferings; and it also tells of our salvation in Christ.

"With His stripes we are healed." There is but one cure for sin and that is in Christ. "And as Moses lifted up the serpent in the wilderness even so must the Son of man be lifted up; that whosoever believeth in Him should not perish, but have eternal life." Back in the days of the lifting of the brazen serpent, all were cured who looked upon it.

"The Lord hath laid on Him the iniquity of us all." "He shall bear their iniquities." In the Scriptures which tell us of our salvation, we find a great fundamental doctrine, the doctrine of substitution. "It is with *His* stripes we are healed." It is upon *Him* that our iniquity has been laid. Salvation becomes yours when you accept the finished work of Christ.

When we hear this wonderful story of Christ, we want to sing,

Hallelujah, what a Saviour!
Who can take a poor lost sinner
Lift him from the miry clay and set him free.
I will ever tell the story,
Shouting, glory, glory, glory
Hallelujah, Jesus ransomed me.

Here is a testimony to Jesus Christ:
"To the artist He is the Chief Cornerstone.

To the astronomer He is the Sun of Righteousness.

To the biologist He is the Life.

To the builder He is the sure Foundation.

To the carpenter He is the Door.

To the doctor He is the Great Physician.

To the farmer He is the Sower and the Lord of Harvest.

To the geologist He is the Rock of Ages.

To the horticulturist He is the True Vine.

To the judge He is the Righteous Judge, the Judge of all men.

To the newspaper man He is the Good Tidings of great joy.

To the philanthropist He is the Unspeakable Gift.

To the sculptor He is the Living Stone.

To the preacher He is the Word of God."

Let us hear also the testimony of other witnesses:

Pharisees, what do you say of Christ? "He eateth with publicans and sinners."

Caiaphas, what have you to say of Him? "He is a blasphemer."

Pilate, what is your opinion? "I find no fault in this Man."

And you, Judas, who have sold your Master for thirty pieces of silver, have you some fearful charge to hurl against Him? "I have sinned in that I have betrayed innocent blood."

And you, Centurion, what do you say of Him? "Truly this was the Son of God."

And you, demons? "He is the Son of God."

John, the Baptist, what think you of Christ? "Behold, the Lamb of God."

And you, John the Apostle? "He is the bright and morning Star."

Peter, what say you of your Master? "Thou art the Christ, the Son of the living God."

And you, Thomas? "My Lord and my God."

Paul, you once persecuted Him, what is your testimony? "I count all things but loss for the excellency of the knowledge of Christ Jesus my Lord."

Angels of Heaven, what think ye of Him? "Unto you is born a Saviour, which is Christ the Lord."

And Thou, Father in Heaven, who knowest all things? "This is My beloved Son, in whom I am well pleased."

Dear friend, accept Him today as your Saviour. Let Him speak peace to your heart. Do it now!

"CHRISTIANS ARE SISSIES"

"Be strong and of a good courage; be not afraid, neither be thou dismayed: for the Lord thy God is with thee whithersoever thou goest" (JOSH. 1:9).

Not long ago I came across a skeptic's statement that "Christians are sissies." The Nazis say that "the Christian faith weakens the moral fiber and makes men childishly dependent. Christians are always decadent."

Ofttimes Christians have been accused of weakness in times of stress and danger. The world's braggarts have always enjoyed poking fun at Christians, and holding up to ridicule the Christian who has displayed the slightest weakness or lack of courage. The Bob Ingersolls and the Clarence Darrows and the Tom Paines have tried to show the world how strong they are, but strength and courage are more than words.

I am not going to argue with the skeptics and infidels. I am going to discuss Christian courage: what it is, and what it does. We need courage in this time—courage to face bullets, courage to open telegrams, courage to face an uncertain and perhaps empty future, courage to face life, and courage to face death.

I

CHRISTIAN COURAGE GLORIFIES GOD

Christians ought to be courageous, so that the enemies of God would have no occasion to sneer and blaspheme. Weakness and cowardice in the Christian always hurt the cause of Christ, while courage glorifies God.

Even the lost world expects the Christian to exhibit courage in the trying hours. When we fail to measure up, great damage is done. The apostle Peter did not help the cause of Christ when he turned coward in the courtyard at the trial of Jesus. He denied and cursed and caused the enemies of Christ to sneer.

A dear sister in middle Tennessee did not glorify God when her aged and invalid mother died. She went to pieces and vowed that she would never go to church again. Non-Christians made light of such weakness.

But, God was glorified when Gideon and three hundred men put to flight the Midianites. God was glorified when Daniel courageously prayed three times a day even when it meant the lions' den. God was glorified by the courage of the apostle Paul who made even the rulers of Rome to tremble. Your courage in hours of stress will glorify God. "Be strong and of a good courage; be not afraid, neither be dismayed."

> Stand up, stand up for Jesus!
> Ye soldiers of the Cross;
> Lift high His royal banner,
> It must not suffer loss:
>
> From victory unto victory
> His army He shall lead,
> Till ev'ry foe is vanquished
> And Christ is Lord indeed.

II

Christian Courage Glorifies and Illuminates the Pages of History

The greatest stories in the world are the accounts of Christian courage; courage to stand true to Christ even in the face of danger. From the time of Christ and the first persecution in Jerusalem to the present, Christian heroism has glorified the pages of sacred and secular history.

If you are inclined to think that Christians lack courage, read Foxe's *Books of Martyrs*. If you need something to give you backbone, read of the suffering and persecution and death of those who have followed Christ. If you believe with the mercenary, selfish crowd that "every man has his price," read the history of those who died rather than say "no" to their faith in Christ.

The parade of Christian martyrs began with Stephen, who was stoned to death by enraged Jews. Two thousand Christians died in the persecution that followed the death of Stephen. James was the next to die. Herod Agrippa ordered his death. When he came to die, his accuser, seeing the courage and bravery of James, threw himself at the apostle's feet and confessed his faith in Christ and then cheerfully put his head on the chopping block and they were beheaded together. This is the way the little band that followed Jesus died. Only John escaped a violent death.

When you think of courage, think of the apostle Paul chained in the Mamertine prison in Rome, awaiting the block; a prison where no light of day entered, where no breath of air stirred, a bed on the rocky floor. And yet Paul started a revival in that prison and wrote inspired words to cheer and instruct us down to this hour. Talk about courage, Paul had it. It almost makes us blush to think of our weakness and timidity.

From A. D. 67 and the reign of Nero to the year 303 there were ten terrible persecutions. Nero contrived many horrible ways to put the Christians to death. Some were sewed into the skins of wild beasts and then worried by savage dogs until they died. Others were dressed in clothing made stiff with wax and then set afire to illuminate Nero's garden.

In the reign of Marcus Aurelius Antoninus (A. D. 162), Polycarp, the outstanding Christian of his time, was put to death. He was tied to a stake and the wood piled about him, but when the fire was started it encircled his body and went over him, but did not touch him. Then the executioner pierced him with a sword and such a quantity of blood poured from his body that the flames were put out. But the Jews in anger built the fire again and burned his body to ashes. During this reign of Marcus Aurelius many Christians were cast into the arena with wild beasts, to be torn apart. Others were broiled alive and then beheaded.

From the year 286, there comes a story to thrill every heart. A legion of soldiers consisting of 6666 men, and every man a Christian, was ordered to take part in the extermination of Christians in the Roman Empire. These men had been reared in Thebes and had been converted to Christianity. They refused to take part in killing Christians. The emperor was so enraged that he ordered every tenth man to be put to death. When this was done, the remainder was ordered to engage in the work of killing Christians. They refused. Again every tenth man was ordered killed, but still they refused to do the emperor's bidding. And then in rage Maximilian ordered the entire legion executed. On September 22, 286, every man died for his faith in Christ.

In the fifteenth century John Huss was put to death for his faith in Christ. He was a young man, 34, when tried and sentenced by the Roman Church. When he was brought to the place of execution, he sang several portions of the Psalms and then looking steadfastly toward Heaven he prayed, "Into Thy hands, O Lord! do I commit my spirit. Thou hast redeemed me, O most good and merciful God."

When the chain was put about him at the

stake, Huss said, with a smiling countenance, "My Lord Jesus Christ was bound with a harder chain than this for my sake, and why then should I be ashamed of this rusty one?" The flames were applied to the faggots and John Huss sang so loudly and so cheerfully that he was heard above the noise of the crackling flames and the multitude.

Time would not permit a review of the courage of many others who fought, suffered, bled and died for Christ: Savonarola, Martin Luther, David Livingstone, John Bunyan, and the thousands of unnamed heros of the faith.

In Germany today where Christianity has been set aside as a weak and decadent religion, men and women are suffering for their faith. Martin Niemoeller has gone through a thousand hells, but his courage has not failed. God wants men of courage! God's work is not done by the masses, nor by systems. It is done by men of courage.

III

Real Courage Comes from Faith in Christ

We need courage to stand true, courage to face life's disappointments and sorrows, courage to face death. God knows this day calls for courage. We do not have to endure sufferings such as others have, but we have difficult and trying days ahead, even upon us now. The men, women and young people without faith in Jesus will be of all people most miserable.

By faith the Christian has a Friend "that sticketh closer than a brother." You have one by your side. You are like the Hebrew children who defied King Nebuchadnezzar. The king said that all should worship a golden image. Shadrach, Meshach, and Abednego said, "Be it known unto thee, O King, that we will not serve thy gods, nor worship the golden image which thou hast set up." This made the king so angry that he commanded the furnace to be heated seven times hotter than usual and the Hebrews cast in. They were bound and cast in, but it was not long until the king began to shake like a leaf in the wind. He said, "We cast in *three men bound*, but lo, I see *four men loose*, walking in the midst of the fire, and they have no hurt, and the form of the fourth is like the Son of God" (Dan. 3:25).

That is the reason the Christian can laugh in the devil's face and smile when sorrows like sea billows roll.

When thro' fiery trials thy pathway shall lie,
My grace, all sufficient, shall be thy supply;
The flames shall not hurt thee; I only design
Thy dross to consume, and thy gold to refine.

By faith the Christian has a God who can be reached by prayer. He has God, Jehovah, Maker of Heaven and earth. Faith in Christ brings us the privilege of prayer. Without faith in Christ you do not have it.

It is not weak to pray, as some would have you to believe. God's great men have always prayed. In hours of stress, pray! God will renew your strength, He will impart to you a new courage to fight life's battles.

By faith the Christian has everlasting life. Therefore, he is indestructible. The world, the flesh, and the devil may test and try, buffet and beat, but the Christian goes on. He has the gift of everlasting life. Heaven is his home. He has the promise of life, eternal life, with God. He is "looking for a city which hath foundations, whose builder and maker is God."

It takes courage to live and it takes courage to die. But if we live, let us live unto the Lord, and if we die, let us die unto the Lord, for in Him is courage, and strength, and victory.